T0123402

EVEN BROKEN CAN BE *beautiful*

A STORY OF LIFE, LOSS, AND THE HOPE OF HEAVEN

Sarah Rieke

WESTBOW
PRESS®
A DIVISION OF THOMAS NELSON
& ZONDERVAN

Unless noted otherwise, all Scripture quotations are taken from The Holy Bible, English Standard Version® (ESV®), Copyright © 2001 by Crossway, a publishing ministry of Good News Publishers. All rights reserved.

Scripture quotations marked NKJV are taken from the New King James Version®. Copyright © 1982 by Thomas Nelson. Used by permission. All rights reserved.

Scripture quotations marked BSB are taken from The Holy Bible, Berean Study Bible, BSB Copyright ©2016, 2018 by Bible Hub. Used by Permission. All Rights Reserved Worldwide.

This book is a work of non-fiction. Unless otherwise noted, the author and the publisher make no explicit guarantees as to the accuracy of the information contained in this book and in some cases, names of people and places have been altered to protect their privacy.

WestBow Press books may be ordered through booksellers or by contacting:

WestBow Press
A Division of Thomas Nelson & Zondervan
1663 Liberty Drive
Bloomington, IN 47403
www.westbowpress.com
1 (866) 928-1240

Because of the dynamic nature of the Internet, any web addresses or links contained in this book may have changed since publication and may no longer be valid. The views expressed in this work are solely those of the author and do not necessarily reflect the views of the publisher, and the publisher hereby disclaims any responsibility for them.

Any people depicted in stock imagery provided by Getty Images are models, and such images are being used for illustrative purposes only. Certain stock imagery © Getty Images.

ISBN: 978-1-9736-5581-7 (sc)
ISBN: 978-1-9736-5580-0 (hc)
ISBN: 978-1-9736-5582-4 (e)

Library of Congress Control Number: 2019902548

Print information available on the last page.

WestBow Press rev. date: 03/19/2019

Sarah Rieke has written one of the most profound and fearless books I have ever read.

Cara Whitney, author of *Unbridled Faith: 100 Devotions from the Horse Farm*

Even Broken Can Be Beautiful is one of the most moving, powerful books I've ever read. I found it impossible to write an endorsement that warrants the justice it deserves. Sarah's devastating journey through every mother's worst nightmare, her painful acceptance of God's will, and the precious heart lessons God taught her through it all had me wiping bitter tears of grief with one hand and sweet tears of joy with the other.

Sarah is a living testimony of what it means to walk through the Valley of the Shadow of Death while learning to trust in God's sovereignty at all costs. Her story, told with such raw emotion, transparency, and vulnerability, is for every woman who has ever questioned the goodness of God and wants to experience His faithfulness in the midst of any tragedy.

Ginger Hubbard, best-selling author of *Don't Make Me Count to Three* and *I Can't Believe You Just Said That!*

Sarah's writing is compelling. God sent me her story at just the right time, my sackcloth and ashes as I grieved the loss of my newly adopted son. After reading this book, I feel as though I've just had coffee with a good friend, a friend whose heart resonates with my grief but, like me, is finding joy in the midst of so much pain.

Cori Salchert, hospice mama and author of *I Will Love You Forever*

Sarah's words so beautifully draw us into her story of both sorrow and redemption, all while pointing us toward the hope we have in Christ. I found myself nodding along and saying "me too" over and over (often tearfully but in the very best way). Her words are both relatable and uplifting to anyone who has walked through suffering.

Kristin Hernandez, blogger at *Sunlight in December* and co-host of *Through the Lens Podcast*

Even Broken Can Be Beautiful is full of the hard-won wisdom that can only come through the most heartbreaking life circumstances. With God-given sensitivity and grace, Sarah writes the story of how she and her husband lost two babies. I found myself weeping and celebrating along with Sarah as I read. Her story of spiritual hardship and growth challenged me to pray through my own spiritual struggles, even though they were very different from Sarah's. Part memoir, part spiritual guidebook, this book will encourage readers as they walk through their own unexpected and heartbreaking journeys and challenge them to embrace both the broken and the beautiful in order to become more like Jesus.

Brittany Meng, author of *Unexpected: Learning to Love Your Unpredictable Story*, blogger at *TheBamBlo*g, and creator and editor of *Mothering Beyond Expectations Collective Blog*

Even Broken Can Be Beautiful is a book of incredible redemption and such sweet hope for heaven. It had me shouting "amen" in every single chapter! Sarah has a gift in how she allows the Lord to use her story to reach women who have walked the road of any type of suffering. I'm thankful for her wisdom in trusting the Lord even in the broken and the beautiful. This book has impacted my heart in so many ways.

Caitlin Mathieu, blogger at *DueToJoy.com*

There is a genuine calmness to Sarah's voice, which comes out through her writing as she shares the parts of her story that are painful and unimaginable. For anyone walking through the pain of losing a child, they will find a voice in this book that is honest, comforting, and sincere. It's a voice that understands, encourages, and challenges them to grab hold of what is true and have the courage to walk forward.

Sarah Bragg, host of *Surviving Sarah Podcast* and author of *Body. Beauty. Boys. The Truth About Girls and How See Ourselves*

As I reflect, mourn, and hope alongside Sarah throughout these words of her testimony, it is clear page after page that this Spirit-filled bereaved mother does not shrink from death but rather, by way of the Holy Spirit can say, "Where, O death, is your sting?" Stories like this need to be told. It is through the telling of testimonies such as Sarah's that the enemy is defeated. What a gift that as members of the body of Christ we get to partner with Sarah in bringing the Kingdom of God to earth, so that it may be on earth as it is in heaven. What a gift that we may surrender our brokenness to be made beautiful by Him, and that the hope of the cross of Christ can touch even our children's earthly graves, providing us with the blessed assurance of reuniting with them in glory.

Holly Colonna, co-host of *Through the Lens Podcast*

Sarah has one of the most genuine hearts of anyone you'll ever meet. Her story is real and raw in every way, and the Lord takes those real and raw parts of her story to create a deeper understanding of who He is. This book will inspire you to shift your perspective towards eternity in a way that we all desperately need.

Alexis Judy, author of *Because He Loved Me*

CONTENTS

FOREWORD

"Though the mountains be shaken
and the hills be removed,
yet my unfailing love for you will not be shaken
nor my covenant of peace be removed,"
says the Lord, who has compassion on you.

—Isaiah 54:10

It was a warm summer evening, and I was the new girl when I met Sarah. My husband had just started a new position as a youth pastor at a new-to-us church in a new-to-us city. The previous few years of my life had been physically and emotionally exhausting. We'd been through infertility, miscarriages, foster parenting, chronic illness, surgeries, and difficult recoveries. A lot of brokenness had defined our life for the previous five years: broken dreams, broken hearts, broken relationships, and broken bodies. As I looked around at all the new people in my life, I felt a large chasm and a struggle to connect.

No one knew our story. How would they react? Would there be a lack of understanding that sometimes naturally comes with not knowing someone during the hardest parts of his or her life? Uncertain and a bit insecure, I nervously attended an outing to a minor-league baseball game with the rest of the youth group leaders. I sat next to my husband and pretended to focus on the game as the other wives chatted with an ease that suggested they'd been friends for a while.

As the daughter of a naval officer, I've done my fair share of moving and starting over. I know all too well how hard it can be to break into already established friend groups, and what I've learned is that all you really need is one good friend. In every city I ever lived, in every season of life, I've known that if I can make just one friend, I'll be okay.

When Sarah turned to me in the middle of the baseball game and asked, "Do you like to craft, Lauren?" she became that friend for me.

Sarah never glossed over or changed the subject when I shared some of the harder parts of my story. She listened and cared, and she usually had chocolate on hand. That's Sarah though, always thinking of others. As our friendship has grown over the last decade, I've learned that she loves others consistently and selflessly in a way that seems to come naturally to her. Even when her heart is breaking, she'll still want to know, "How are you doing? Are things okay with you?" As she moves through life, with all of its broken beauty, she does so with an eye on her neighbors and what she might offer us.

When Sarah lost her daughter Evie and subsequently her son Charlie, her world turned upside down and inside out. Safe and sacred things shattered. She had to learn how to view and live in the brokenness of life on earth while still clinging to the hope and beauty of heaven. Instead of turning inward, drawing the shades, and bolting the doors against an often-cruel world, Sarah opened her arms and her heart. She's flung open her soul for the benefit of all of us who have ever had our dreams shattered and hopes trampled … to show us that we aren't alone and that broken can really be beautiful.

Sarah's story, shared as a love offering in this book, is a testament to the unfailing love, unbreakable peace, and unending compassion of our Father in heaven. My hope for you, dear reader, is that you will find Sarah in these pages, much as I did nearly ten years ago at that baseball game … a gentle, loving, and generous friend who offers hope and empathy as we move through this broken and beautiful life.

Lauren Casper, author of *It's Okay About It*

INTRODUCTION

It was mid-November. The air was crisp but comfortable, and the sun shone down from a cloudless sky onto the group of us gathered under the dark green tent below.

I sat in the very middle of the first and only row of chairs underneath that tent, my husband to my right. And directly in front of us laid a tiny ivory casket with white and cream marbling, not three feet long, covered in a bouquet of roses and carnations in varying shades of pink. A handmade white tulle butterfly dotted with iridescent sequins was tucked carefully among the flowers. For what it was, it was beautiful.

Inside that tiny casket lay the reason we were all gathered there that lovely November morning, the reason for the oceans of tears and sleepless nights, and the reason for the deeper understanding I now held of life with limits and life eternal.

Inside that casket was my daughter.

This day—this funeral day—was the culmination of weeks of dreaded anticipation of losing my baby daughter since the grim day four months prior when we learned of her fatal diagnosis in a routine ultrasound. She had been labeled "incompatible with life." And every day for four months, I carried that death sentence with me, all while trying desperately to live this story in the best way I could for the God who wrote it for me, the God who tenderly held my hand all along the way.

I will never forget the weight of those four months and how I had to be so deliberate each and every day to plant my feet firmly on the floor and continue living my life when everything inside me wanted to melt away into a puddle of hot tears. I wanted to run—nowhere in particular but very fast and very far away to a fictional place where my reality was not my own. I will never forget how exhaustingly intentional I had to be to keep my mind focused on Christ and the truths of God's Word and not allow myself to slink into the deep, dark depression that heinously beckoned. And I will never, ever forget changing from the person I was before to the person I have become since.

Sitting beneath that tent on that particular Saturday in November, I felt something I cannot fully describe. There underneath that funeral tent, surrounded by loved ones and staring at the casket of the daughter I would never really know, I felt God's presence. While the sounds of our dear friends' voices singing the sweetest a capella renditions of my favorite hymns filled my ears, I felt it. I closed my eyes and let the cool autumn breeze dance across my face, and I leaned in. I leaned into the One who had orchestrated this moment since the beginning of time, since before even one man walked on the earth or a single beam of starlight radiated across the night sky. Before even then, this moment was. And I felt it. I felt the deep, deep beauty in the midst of this heart-wrenching broken.

In that moment of true brokenness was the beauty of God's never-ending love for my child, for me, and ultimately for all of us. That moment revealed an existence of so much more detail to my story than just the pain and sadness of right then, but a bigger, more universal story of redemption and the hope of an eternity with all things new. And three years later, it was the comfort of that same promise of an eternity with all things new that carried me through another loss, another baby gone, another child I would not know until heaven.

I don't know what brokenness has brought you here today or what has led you to crack open the pages of this book, but I do know the God who is sovereign over all things, even our brokenness. And I know this God to be a good, good Father who wants good things for His children and will not put one more ounce of hardship into our lives than it will take to precisely conform us to the image of His precious Son, Jesus.

Pain is the worst, and as humans, we do everything we can to avoid it. Avoid pain; pursue comfort, ease, and anything chocolate-covered.

That's our creed ... or at least mine anyway. But I stand firmly on the solid rock of truth on which I've had to cling with the tips of my fingernails many times, and proclaim this truth: there is nothing—absolutely nothing—that cannot become beautiful because of our Father who works all things for our benefit and for the benefit and furtherance of His kingdom.

This is my story, which is, in essence, a story of losing babies. But it is really so much more than that. It is the story of a kind God laying up a storehouse of truth within a heart that He loves—truth that would sustain when life suddenly felt unsurvivable. It is the story of a heart bending to the Lord's will even when nothing made sense—arguably *because* nothing else made sense. It is the story of a heart becoming well-acquainted with the messiness of grief. It is the story of putting flesh on the bones of my faith, of muscle built from the exertion of wrestling with questions I thought we were never allowed to ask. It is the story of finding hope in Jesus in an otherwise hopeless mess. It is the story of surrendering to God's omnipotent nature and His divine pen that writes every detail of every story played out here on earth. And ultimately it is the story of how, in Christ, all of these hard things—these messy things, these ugly things, these desperate things, and these broken things in our lives—can be made beautiful.

PART I

LAYERS OF TRUTH FOR MY HEART

THIS LIFE IS NOT
ALL THERE IS

Q: What is the chief end of man?
A: Man's chief end is to glorify God, and to enjoy Him forever.[1]

—The Westminster Shorter Catechism

The idea of heaven had always been a bit scary to me. It was not as scary as the prospect of spending an eternity in a lake of fire, I suppose (which is why I made a profession of faith at a young age), but still scary.

As a kid, anytime I tried to imagine heaven, a sinking feeling would creep into the pit of my stomach. Most of the time it would happen as I lay in my bed in the dark, trying to fall asleep. I would start to think about heaven and the idea of being somewhere forever and ever with no end, where time as I knew it no longer existed. And then I would begin to sweat, and tears would well up in the corners of my eyes. I would feel that familiar rock-pit feeling invade my insides. I wanted so much to figure out this whole heaven thing, to figure out what forever actually meant, but I could not grasp it. Instead of ending with comforting conclusions, my questions left my chest heaving with nervous gulps of air and my soul gaping with discomfort over the unknown. What would my life be like after I left this one?

Even as a kid, I knew that death was a part of life. My mom often talked about her experience with death as a seven-year-old girl watching her beloved mother lose a years-long battle with cancer. My mom recounted memories of caring for her dying mother, catching buckets of her blood-filled vomit, running outside to empty them, and returning just in time for the buckets to be filled again.

You can imagine then how death and dying held such painful connotations for my mom. She hated thinking about it. Any conversation surrounding death turned her eyes small and fearful, as if even just the word itself sucked a little life out of her soul.

My mom loved her adult life, the existence she built with her husband and two daughters. It was so vastly different from the grief-laden life she left behind as a child, and she certainly did not want to dwell on the memories that caused her such deep wounds. In her mind, nothing could be better than the life she had raising her own little family whom she loved fiercely.

One night before bed, my mom opened up to me about what it was like to lose her mother at such a young age. She shared about how sad life was after her mother had passed away. She talked about how much she missed having a mother during her growing-up years and now how much she missed not having maternal guidance for her own motherhood journey. I stared at my mom's long, shimmery red fingernails as she wiped a tear off her cheek.

"It's just so hard," she said. "Death is so hard."

Eight-year-old me tried my best to comfort my mother. "But there's heaven!" I piped up. "Heaven will be good, right?"

"Yeah, it's true," she continued, "but it won't be the same."

My mom's voice trailed off, as if contemplating all the wonderful things of this world she wished she could scoop up and take with her into eternity.

That brief conversation clung like a magnet to my childlike mind. From that point on, my mom's fear that heaven would not be as good as life here on earth formed the basis for everything I understood about my heavenly eternity: it would be a less-than version of my life here on earth. Part of my anxieties about the afterlife included the idea that even in heaven there would remain inside of me a deep longing for the life I left behind on earth. That sounded awful to me. Who wants to spend eternity wishing he or she were someplace else? This misconception even followed me into adulthood and continued to shape the way I viewed life after death. But all of that changed one night many years later, with one very pointed conversation with my husband.

At the time, Josh was a night-shift nurse in the intensive care unit at our local hospital. Death was truly part of the job. The patients on that ICU floor were the sickest of the sick. Most of the patients were intubated and hooked up to ventilators because they were unable to breathe independently. Josh regularly responded to codes, which meant that a patient's heart had stopped beating, and the medical team had to use resuscitation measures to keep that person alive. And though he and the medical staff would do the best they could to keep the patient's heart beating, sometimes they were unable to.

Despite these crazy-intense moments, Josh said the hardest part of his job was not dealing with the life-threatening illnesses or horrific injuries but rather the patients' families. They were often demanding and unable to fully comprehend their family member's delicate health state. Time and time again, family requested aggressive medical treatment for these severely ill and suffering patients whose bodies were failing and who had no reasonable expectation of returning to any quality of life. Because they were required to carry out these requested aggressive medical treatments, Josh and the other staff often felt as though they were prolonging the patient's misery, causing them additional and needless pain and suffering in their last days.

Josh would also have regular interactions with the family members of newly deceased patients, and he was often in the room with the patient and their family the moment the patient passed away. Raised in a pastor's family, my husband had a solid foundation in Jesus and was a key member in our local church. He was certainly no cynic toward spiritual things. But he said he hated that it was often the newly bereaved Christian families who seemed to display the worst coping behaviors after their family member passed away.

Josh replayed for me two very impressionable experiences in the ICU. He told me about one family who had surrounded their dying loved one, hands joined and prayers and praise raised to heaven. When the patient passed away, the family members did not handle the news well and began screaming, turning over furniture, and creating all sorts of disturbances on the ICU floor. Their behavior escalated to the point that the staff had to call security to escort the family safely out of the building.

Another time, a local pastor's wife lay dying of cancer. This devoted husband gently stroked his wife's hand as her soul flew to Jesus. But when it came time for his wife's body to be taken away, he refused and asked for the nursing staff to leave her body in the room for three days so she could be resurrected, as Jesus was. Of course the staff was unable to carry out this request. The husband eventually relented, but not without some considerable resistance. These two experiences, among others, left such an impression on Josh's mind.

Certainly he understood the delicate emotional state of these family members left behind in the cruel wake of death. The finality of death is incredibly difficult to face, and some handle it better than others. Death unveils an intimidating depth of emotional vulnerability and a blistering awareness of our own human fragility. It makes sense that death would elicit such a deeply emotional response. But despite the intense grief and shock of death, believers *are* called to act differently in the face of this type of adversity. "But we do not want you to be uninformed, brothers, about those who are asleep, that you may not grieve as others who have no hope" (1 Thessalonians 4:13).

Believers in Christ are called to grieve differently because we have hope.

That night Josh told me something that changed me forever. He told me that as Christians, our lives on earth are just not that important. Not that we should move toward emotional despair or feelings of cosmic insignificance. Rather that, if we truly believe what we say we believe about the perfect eternity that Jesus offers through salvation in

Him, we should face death in this life with all the hope of that eternal reality. If we truly believe what we say we do about heaven, then we know full well that this life is not all there is to our soul's existence.

The apostle Paul manifested this truth in his own life. "For to me to live is Christ, and to die is gain. If I am to live in the flesh, that means fruitful labor for me. Yet which I shall choose I cannot tell. I am hard pressed between the two. My desire is to depart and be with Christ, for that is far better."[2]

Honestly, I was initially offended at Josh's statement, imagining that it meant he would not feel even the slightest twinge of sadness if I died. He assured me that was absolutely not the case. But the truth was, if death separated the two of us in this earthly life far sooner than we anticipated, it would not be the end of our relationship. Drawing on the assurance of heaven that our salvation through Jesus offers, we would each have the hope of seeing one another again on the perfect shores of eternity, reunited and reconciled to God in the way He always meant for us to be.

In the beginning, God's intention was for His people, His image-bearers, to live in a perfect world, a lush utopia in the garden of Eden. But when man chose to give in to the temptation of the enemy, sin entered into the world, and all the perfection that was originally intended by the Father disintegrated.

Sin separated God from His people. But God did not want it to stay that way. Instead He authored a plan that would allow the restoration of the souls of His people, so that one day they could be reunited. And the way He did this was through the work of His Son, Jesus.

Jesus Christ died on a rugged wooden cross for our sins and then rose again after being dead for three days. Jesus died to make a way for anyone who chooses to believe—for anyone who accepts this redeeming work—as a way back to the Father. In Christ, the end of this life here on earth is only the beginning of something new. Christ conquered death and, in doing so, made a way for anyone in Him to do the same. Herein lies our hope.

This hope is what allows believers to grieve differently. Will we be grieved? Yes of course. But not as those with no hope of heaven, no hope of eternity, and no hope of being reunited with loved ones in the most perfect place forever. It is important for believers to live well on this earth to bring glory to God, but this life is not all there is. There is a life after this one, and it should change the way we view death.

These thoughts had never really occurred to me before that night. What Josh described to me felt truly groundbreaking, a grand illumination where there was once darkness. It was headline news to my heart that had never really considered how the hope of heaven could change the way I viewed losing loved ones here on earth.

But there was one aspect of heaven that I still didn't understand, one that still felt slightly awkward and uncomfortable, like wearing a wet woolen sweater. What remained was the doubt that heaven was something to look forward to. Were there good things there? Enjoyable things? In that same conversation, I was finally brave enough to ask Josh the question that had been pushing and prying to come out, but for the fear that kept it contained.

I ashamedly blurted out to him that I thought life in heaven would not be as good as life here on earth, half-hoping he wouldn't really hear me. Or maybe, like the telephone game when you were a kid, it would sound like something totally different by the time it reached his ears.

Much to my chagrin, he heard me with distinct clarity. His eyes widened. "Of course heaven will be better than earth!" he exclaimed.

I nodded sheepishly and continued to listen as Josh assured me that heaven would be infinitely better than any day I'd ever experienced on earth—like the best days I'd ever lived, only better. Heaven would be the feeling of newness that comes from watching the sky turn from dark to soft watercolor blues as morning breaks. Heaven would be climbing into the best corner of the couch with a blanket and a good book and finally breathing a sigh of deep relaxation. Heaven would be heart-to-heart talks, deep belly laughs, and whispers shared between friends, all with pure love and joy and not a hint of worry for things to come. Heaven would be every good thing and every good feeling forever and without any trace of the fall.

It took a little while for these new thoughts to assimilate into my brain. I had never before considered what it would be like to live an existence untainted by sin. Most certainly it *would* be better than life here because even our sweetest moments in this life are brushed with little traces of the fall, of what happened after man chose to sin.

Up until that point, I had imagined heaven as a less fun place where you went after you died. And maybe, since you were so spiritually perfect or whatever once you got there, you wouldn't mind all the harp playing and sitting around, singing things to God. I had never thought of heaven as the absolute best moments of this life, free from any stain of sin and forever.

A foreverness of my favorite days, I could live with that. The thought freed me. It was labored breathing replaced with a deeply cleansing sigh. What once filled me with a sense of dread now brought contented anticipation of what heaven would hold. These thoughts were transforming me, altering the way I thought about life forever in the presence of the Lord.

One evening a few weeks later, I was home alone, sweeping up leftover crumbs from dinner. As I worked the tiny bits of food and dust into a neat little pile, I pondered and prayed. I thought about that night and that discussion with Josh. I thought about the reality that death would come one day and heaven very soon after.

Instead of feeling a sense of uncertainty and dismay for what the life after this one had to offer, the thought of going to a truly wonderfully perfect place after death now gave me comfort. It gave me hope that if a born-again loved one were to die, he or she would be in that perfect place, and we would see each other again. Fear and misunderstanding had been replaced with understanding and peace.

I felt the Lord leading me to pray.

Lord, if anything ever happens to Josh, if he dies much sooner than expected, I wouldn't hold it against You. Help me to still give You the glory and see his death for what it means in light of Your eternity.

It was more than a prayer really. It was a promise. My heart had truly been changed. I was not afraid of losing my husband, should the Lord decide to take him from me. At the time, that was my worst-case scenario, but I meant every word.

The Lord seared these thoughts and prayers deeply into my heart. It was as if He placed every new thing I now knew and felt about heaven into a little satin satchel and pressed it into the softest part of my palm, closing my fingers around it as if to say, "Hold onto these, Beloved. You will need them one day soon."

Broken

Death is a horribly inescapable reality in this world, a result of the sin that entered after the fall of man in the garden of Eden.

Beautiful

God has made a way for us to all spend eternity in heaven with Him, a way made possible to those who accept the saving work of His Son Jesus. And this heaven will be a place where there will be no more tears and no more pain, filled only with peace and perfection, a wonderful place to look forward to.

HE CAME TO GIVE ABUNDANT LIFE

[Jesus] has never stopped longing to give us all we need. He has never stopped *being* all we need. He comes in and makes our days and lives mean something. He brings all the joy and excitement— more than we could ask or imagine.[1]

—Jess Connolly

My life circa 2008 was good. There was really nothing to complain about. I had a solid marriage and a great husband, and we had a cute 1950s-era bungalow starter home. We were very involved in our church as leaders in the youth ministry, Josh as the worship leader and I as one of the primary leaders for the teen girls. We both had great jobs and a steady income. We were working really hard to pay down our undergrad loans, and it was proving to be quite a successful endeavor. We had a handful of dear friends who lived very close by, and we would get together with them regularly for pizza, games, movies, and conversations that would keep us talking well past what anyone would consider a reasonable bedtime. Life was very good.

And yet …

Even in the midst of all of these good things, my heart longed for something more. Well actually, not just something as in *anything* more. A baby sort of more. My heart longed to be a mother, to carry and birth a baby and to care for that sweet little child with everything in me. I ached deeply inside for a baby of my very own.

To add insult to injury, I was the only woman in my circle of friends who did not have children. It seemed like I was surrounded by young mothers and their cute little babies and toddlers. And these mothers seemed to have all the time in the world to get together for playdates and women's Bible study group, all the while I was stuck in my nine-to-five job, stuck in my childless life.

Honestly, what felt most difficult during that time was that every conversation my friends had seemed to be centered on motherhood in some way. They would swap birth stories and postpartum recovery horror stories. They would sympathize with one another over babies with stomach flu and babies with acid reflux so severe it seemed like they had the stomach flu. They would empathetically nod their heads with one another while describing, play-by-play, yet another sleepless night. I would attempt to chime in and somehow relate my life experiences to theirs, but my attempts at creating those parallels felt so hollow measured up against their full and abounding lives.

One evening in late summer, I had the idea to invite my friends over to my house for a kid-free barbecue. The Bible says that if you want friends, you must show yourself to be friendly, and so that was my plan. I would invite a handful of ladies over, and we could chat over grilled chicken, charred corn on the cob, and juicy, almost overripe summer tomatoes. And since it was at my house and I had no children, I imagined that meant that no one would talk about their kids, even a little. In my mind, it was the perfect plan.

The dinner was really lovely. We decided to go sort of potluck style, and my favorite dish that night was a creamy corn casserole. But somewhere in between our last bites of tomato-basil salad and the first bites of dessert, I realized that nothing about this night was different. I was sitting in my own space at my own kitchen table in silence, while the girls around me flurried in conversation over toddler milestones and husband-to-wife diaper-changing ratios.

Tears collected in the corners of my eyes, and I fought to keep them from spilling over onto my cheeks. I had wanted this night to feel so different, for me to finally feel like a real part of the group, even if it were just this once. But I still felt so very much the same. Even among friends, I still felt the sharp pang of loneliness. All of my friends were on this island called motherhood, laughing, chatting, and freely relating to one another's lives. And I was alone on an island nearby, watching and longing to occupy the same beach they did, the stretch of sand that represented everything I wanted to be.

A short time after the dinner party that fell woefully short of my expectations, I had a very tear-filled conversation with my husband where I begged and begged and, with a significant lack of dignity, begged some more for a baby. I pleaded with him to reconsider the family plan that we had decided on long before we ever said "I do." It was the plan that would allow Josh to finish his master's degree but would require me to work him through school. What this plan would most decidedly not allow was for me to become a stay-at-home mom to our own precious bundle.

We talked back and forth for quite some time—me trying to convince Josh that we should abandon our original plan and him trying to remind me of exactly why we had set the whole plan up in the first place. Eventually I imagine it was his pure frustration over the whole ordeal that caused Josh to throw his hands up and reluctantly relent to my pleas.

I was so excited at first. My tears and sobs gave way to a triumphant and excited smile. But that emotional high came crashing down the next day. Deep in my heart, I knew I had gone about this whole thing the wrong way. I wanted a baby so badly, but I did not want a baby without my husband's heart being all in. My heart ached so badly to belong that I lost sight of our long-term goals. I lost sight of the purpose God had for me right then.

And so the next day, I swallowed my pride, apologized for letting my emotions create a desperate monster out of me, and told Josh that I would wait, as originally planned, for motherhood. But I was desperately unhappy, unfulfilled, and bitterly dissatisfied.

Every single day I felt a sick pull at the pit of my stomach and had the sense that the days I was living, sans babies, were just a waste of life. These days simply seemed to be a holding tank for the one glorious day when the gate would swing wide open and I could walk into my actual, happy life, filled with all the chubby babies I could stand. This in-between waiting phase left me with an uncomfortable empty longing. My spirit bubbled with discontentment.

After many months of living this way, I reached a point where I was actually quite sick of my own disgruntled heart. Surely I wasn't meant to spend my days this way? Surely life could mean something in these years in between marriage and starting a family? There had to be something I was missing. The Lord would soon help me find that missing piece.

One morning I drove to work. The blur of the road and the passing street signs mirrored the blur of thoughts inside my head. I was once again dwelling on everything I didn't have, and it sickened me. In an attempt to interrupt that negative thought pattern, I turned on some music. A song I'd heard dozens of times before began to play. The familiar female voice sang familiar words, but I heard them this time with new clarity, my discontented heart drinking up the truth and the challenge of every line.

> You make me want to live.
> You make me want to live.
> You came to shake us,
> And to wake us up to something more,
> Than we'd always settled for,
> And you make me want to live.[2]

The heart of the message of this song comes from John 10:10, in which Jesus declares that He came to give us life and to give us life abundantly. Living from a place of abundance had certainly not been my standard operating procedure at that point in time. Instead I had been living from a place of scarcity, disappointment, and wishing everything could be vastly different than it was. In doing so, I was robbing myself of the riches of these days and this life. In essence, I was living spitefully toward Jesus, who made the ultimate sacrifice so I could live my days to the fullest of His calling in my life.

My dream of becoming a mother did not go away that day, but I was overcome with a new determination. I was on a newfound mission to live these in-between days the best way I could, to the glory of the Son of God who died so I could live. I asked the Lord to forgive my spirit of ungratefulness and discontentment, did an about-face, and vowed never to turn back.

I walked into my office at work that day armed with new resolve. No longer would I live with a sense that all I had to look forward to were the days far into the future when I could become a stay-at-home mom. That day I purposed myself to live out the days right before me, the days my feet were presently standing in. Jesus did not pay the price for my life for me to wallow in unhappiness and dissatisfaction. Jesus came that I might live life and that I might live it abundantly.

There are so many situations where we place our lives on hold for something we desperately want. We are paralyzed from doing this, making these plans, or counting on this thing until we have the house, the boyfriend, the car, the job. But Jesus Christ came so we could live abundantly right where we are. We don't have to wait for the next thing in order for our lives to have great purpose. We don't have to wait for the next big life moment in order for our lives to have meaning. Our lives have deep purpose and meaning in this present moment.

Certainly this does not exempt us from setting goals and striving to reach them. It is more than okay to want to land that perfect career, marry that Prince Charming, or live out the American dream with the average 1.25 children. Part of the beauty of our freedom in Christ is that we have gifts, talents, and abilities that He has granted to us and that equip us for His very special purpose for our lives. Goal setting is more than okay. What is not okay, however, is putting our lives on hold until we achieve those goals, living as if the days until we reach that goal are meaningless. They are absolutely quite the opposite of that.

I once had a conversation with a young woman who felt like her life was absolutely worthless because she was not married. She felt as though her life would not really begin until she had a ring on her finger and a husband to come home to every day. To prove a point, I presented her with a hypothetical question. I asked her what would happen if she didn't get married for ten more years. What would she do with those years? Would she really spend ten years of her life thinking that each one of those 3,650 days were completely useless? Certainly that is no way to live.

We can find Rachel, of the infamous Jacob-Leah-Rachel love triangle, saying essentially the same thing. In Genesis 29–30, we see Leah bearing child after child for her husband, Jacob. But at the same time Leah was birthing many sons, Jacob's other wife, Rachel, struggled to conceive. In Genesis 30:1, Rachel cries out to her husband in desperation, "Give me children, or I shall die!" It's definitely dramatic. But gosh, do I know the feeling!

How many times do I feel dead in some way because God does not give me the thing I want at that very moment? How many times do I rob myself of the gift Jesus gave me when He came and died to offer abundant life because I am so focused on what I do not have rather than what He gives me? And what He gives me is assurance of a life full of purpose simply because I am His creation. I am not to find contentment in my circumstances but rather in who I know God to be. Sometimes the very presence of those unfulfilled longings is exactly what I need to draw me close to the heart of God, to seek Him alone.

As Lysa Terkeurst writes, "Each time I feel my heart being pulled down into the pit of ungratefulness and grumbling, I can recognize it as a call to draw near to the Lord. I thank Him for the empty places, for they remind me that only He has the ability to fill me completely."[3]

Months after my heart awakening, I was shoulder to shoulder with my dear friend Justina as we walked down a quaint little street in the middle of The Square in Gainesville, Georgia. We had spent the last few hours catching up and shopping together, admiring all the adorable little trinkets in the local shops.

As we walked, my dear friend, who knew my heart well and had known of my struggle, asked me if I were doing all right. She asked if I were really feeling okay with where I stood in my season of waiting to become a mother.

I hesitated a bit before answering. I wanted to make sure I could answer her with complete honesty. "Yes." I replied, "I really do feel good with waiting."

I still wanted to be a mother very much. It felt like my life's calling. But the Lord had shown me that He died to give me life that was worth living, even in the in-between. I was committed to wait to become a mother. Not only was I committed to wait, but to wait well. I wanted to enjoy all the days up until that point and not just stare out the window, watching my life go by.

Another big heart change came when I decided not only to wait well and enjoy my life as it was, but also to fully engage and celebrate the lives of my friends who were living what I envisioned to be the dream life. No longer did I sulk when we got together and no one asked about my week at work. Instead I initiated conversation about my friends' kids and their lives, and I tried to glean bits of wisdom from them to use one day with my own family. My life wasn't perfect, but I felt a deep sense of contentment, shiny and new.

My heart still longed very much for a baby of my own, but I had learned how to live well despite not having my heart's greatest desire. A baby could not provide the same heart satisfaction that comes only from resting in God's present purpose for my life. At that time, His present purpose for me was to wait patiently and to stay faithful to my job, my husband, my service, and my friends.

I felt as though I had a little taste of what Paul described in Philippians 4:11, of learning how to be content in all things and in all life circumstances. And I am so thankful the Lord allowed me to take that lesson to heart when life was relatively simple because just a few years down the road, I would have to figure out how to have a contented heart even while it was breaking.

Broken

Life often does not give us the exact things we want when we want them, and sometimes we live as if our lives are on hold until those things are achieved.

Beautiful

Christ came so we could live an abundant life right here, right now, no matter our life circumstances.

3

TRUST GOD'S TURNS FOR YOUR LIFE

I don't have magic formulas. All I know is that the
Giver of all good things wouldn't allow you to be in
your current environment today unless it brings you
to a better tomorrow.[1]

—Kristen Strong

The spring semester before Josh and I were married, we began hunting
for apartments. We were looking for something close to the school and
very affordable, a factor that was extremely important considering our
meager income.

One afternoon I noticed a bright yellow flyer on the giant
corkboard just outside of one of the big stadium-type classrooms. It
was an advertisement for an apartment over the detached garage of
one of the most beloved professors on campus. The rent was quite
affordable, and the apartment was near to the school. I immediately
called to inquire on its availability, and the professor's wife told me that
it would definitely be available for rent for the upcoming fall semester.

I was absolutely elated. No sooner had I hung up the phone than I started daydreaming of the life Josh and I would start together in that sweet little apartment. I was also really looking forward to potentially building a mentor-type relationship with the professor and his wife and imagined all the conversations we'd have around the dinner table, laughing together as we sorted through some of our newlywed challenges and smiling as they reminisced with stories of their own. It seemed like the perfect situation for us.

A couple weeks later, however, the professor's wife called me to let me know the renters who were currently residing in the apartment had actually decided to stay and that the space would not be available for rent as she had previously thought. Of course she apologized, and of course I was very polite and ensured her that it was no problem. In my mind, however, it was actually a very big problem.

Disappointment flooded my insides. I already had my heart set on that little place, and now it was gone. It felt like such a strange and unnecessary turn of events. If we weren't meant to have that apartment, why on earth did God allow me down the path of thinking it would be ours? Why did He even allow me to see that flyer in the first place? I was dreadfully disappointed over the loss of the apartment. But even scarier, I felt an extreme sense of disappointment toward the Lord for not allowing us to have what I deemed to be the most perfect little starter apartment for the most perfect little couple.

I spent a couple of days walking around with the unmistakable feeling that God had somehow betrayed me, shortchanged me, held out on me. But eventually He laid hold of my heart and convicted me of this sin of letting my disappointment over the loss of this apartment come in between my relationship with Him. God was faithful to forgive me, of course, but I still felt disappointed that the little place was not going to be ours. As the weeks and months went on, that disappointment faded into a purely genuine curiosity for what that journey had been all about.

About six months later, Josh and I were sitting together in our newlywed apartment. It was different than the one I had wanted, but still very adorable. Even the bright-green shag carpet was beginning to grow on me. We sat at the kitchen table in deep conversation over how to work out the logistics of the next several weeks of the semester with our singular car.

As a nursing student, one very big part of Josh's education was his clinical rotations at the local hospital. Classes on campus were an important part of mine. We only had one car, and that particular upcoming semester, we each needed to be in a different place at the same time.

Previously our schedules coordinated perfectly, allowing us to drive to campus together in the morning and then leave together in the late afternoons after each of us finished our classes. Or Josh had been able to drop me off, use the car to head to the hospital for his clinical shift, and then pick me back up. But the next several weeks presented a change in schedules that we could no longer accommodate as easily. He would have to be at the hospital at the same time I would need to be on campus for classes and then work. The sum of all the parts did not add up to a simple conclusion.

After a little brainstorming, Josh proposed the idea that I could take the car and drive myself to work and class, and he could just ride his bike to the hospital for his shift. When I was done on campus, I would head to the hospital to pick him up. I was a little hesitant at first for Josh to ride his bicycle across the busy road, but he assured me it would be fine. We settled on that as the final plan for the rest of that semester.

A couple of weeks later as I was driving to the hospital to pick Josh up, I was thinking about our little arrangement and how nicely it had worked out. I recalled the memory of that first apartment and how desperately I had wanted it and then how devastated I was when we weren't able to secure it as our own. And then a little light switch in my head illuminated what had once been a dark spot, shrouded by the sense that I knew pretty well how to run my life apart from divine direction. I tangibly sensed how false that confidence was.

If everything had worked out for that first apartment, if we had become renters to that professor and his kind wife, we would have been much farther away from the hospital, much too far for Josh to safely ride his bike. Because God knew the whole story and the exact predicament that would present itself in the last few weeks of that first fall semester as a married couple, He led us away from the apartment that would not have been as good of a fit as the one we ended up with. His infinite kindness and wisdom allowed us to shift our attention from that first apartment choice to the little place on Fort Avenue that we called home.

Suddenly I felt so infinitesimally small in the wake of God's infinite omnipotence, the way a tiny krill might feel swimming in the ocean next to the majesty of a blue whale. Tears of repentance soon followed, and my heart was so grieved that I had not trusted in the God that assured me in His Word that, just as He does for the sparrow, He would always faithfully provide for my needs.

God knew where our lives were going to take us that first semester and purposefully redirected us when we headed down the way that would not be most beneficial for us in the near future. The gift of hindsight allowed me to see that. And it was a precious lesson to hold onto a few years later when our life presented us with another unexpected turn.

Early in 2010, I walked up our driveway after a long drive home from work, my bags in my arms. As I walked up the cinder block steps, Josh unexpectedly opened the door. He was holding a letter in his hand.

"I got a letter from the grad program today," he said with a smile.

"You did!" My eyes grew wide. "Annnnndddd ...?"

Before Josh graduated high school, I remember standing in his kitchen with him, his mom, and his Uncle Brad as they all discussed potential career paths Josh might be interested in pursuing. Brad himself was interested in a nursing career, and so it was the first potential area of study that entered the suggestion pool. A career in nursing offered great job opportunities directly out of undergrad, with the potential of pursuing an advanced nursing degree after a few years of hospital experience.

From the moment Josh walked onto his college campus as a freshman, he had a very singular goal in mind, to earn his bachelor's degree in nursing, work the recommended two years in a general intensive care unit, and then begin the application process for various nurse anesthesia programs. His ultimate goal was to become a certified registered nurse anesthetist (CRNA). This had been his game plan, his career blueprint since day one. When I saw him standing at the door that day, I knew the letter he held was more than just mail. It was a ticket to his future.

In his hands, Josh held the culmination of everything he had worked toward for the last several years. That letter was the gate to his dream, and it would tell us if and when he could start the CRNA program that had been his goal since high school. I was so excited for him.

Honestly though, what I was most excited about was that this letter would provide for me the very tangible countdown until I could achieve my own dream of starting our family. On the advice of wise counsel, Josh and I decided to postpone starting our family until after he finished his master's degree. So this letter was not only the ticket to his career dreams, but my own maternal dreams as well. Nothing could have prepared me for what the few simple lines of print inside that letter would tell us.

"The program is canceled," Josh stated abruptly.

"What?" I blurted out. My mind was buffering, and my mental processing page wasn't loading up quite right.

"The school is reconfiguring the anesthesia program for accreditation reasons," Josh continued, "so they are not accepting a class for this upcoming school year." The corners of his mouth pulled into a sheepish grin, and he let out a quiet chuckle, the way you do when you have full expectation that if you don't chuckle, the likelihood is very high that you might scream ... or cry ... or both.

I was shocked. In my mind, this particular letter could have read in one of two ways:

1. Yes! You have been accepted. Congratulations. Go buy your books and all the things and hunker down for a super-intense twenty-eight months *or*

2. No, I am sorry. We have not accepted your application at this time. Here is your complimentary pint of Ben and Jerry's.

Those were the two scenarios I had in mind. I had not anticipated this weird third option that now hung in the air like a hazy cloud, taunting us with its vague ambivalence.

Scenario one would have been ideal obviously. Josh would have been able to start the program in the fall and be well on his way to achieving his career goal. Scenario two would have been less ideal because rejection is rarely the go-to choice for the human species, but at least it would have allowed us to explore other options and alternative schools.

But this third thing? This weird, unexpected third thing left us in a place of ambiguity and uncertainty as to what our expectation should be for this program at this particular school and our family's future. Were we supposed to wait and see if the program would become reaccredited and accept students for the following year? Were we supposed to apply to other schools and face the prospect of moving away? Were we supposed to see this as a sign and just keep doing what we were doing for an indefinite period of time?

In my mind, everything was now completely up in the air. We had just been thrown a curve ball that I wasn't ready for. Actually it felt more like being at home plate, with your hands gripping the bat and arms ready to swing when the coach runs up to tell you that you're actually supposed to be playing basketball. And then you look down at your cleats and wonder how exactly you are supposed to make the transition to the basketball court when you were clearly ready for the baseball field. You were ready for baseball, not basketball.

I was not ready for basketball.

But what I may have been even less prepared for were the words that came out of Josh's mouth next.

"You know," he started slowly, "this means we don't have to put off having a baby."

I looked at him, just as shocked as I had been when he told me the program had been canceled. We sat on the couch and talked for a while, my emotions ping-ponging between disappointment and disbelief—disappointment that Josh's dream was oddly put on hold and disbelief that mine might be just within arm's reach.

Josh explained that he wasn't really willing to put off having a family for some unspecified amount of time for this program that may or may not ever have its accreditation restored. Becoming a nurse anesthetist was his goal, yes, but what he ultimately wanted was to have a family.

I was stunned. I could hardly let myself believe this could be happening. The thing I had wanted for so long was right here at my fingertips. It felt too good to be true.

Since this was only Monday, Josh and I decided to pray separately on this issue for the rest of the week and then come together and talk about it again on Friday. It was a good, solid plan, and so I agreed.

At the start of the week I was oddly against this idea. It was as if the complete freedom I felt allotted in making this decision to start our family paralyzed me. Was this really what we should do? Was this the right decision or just the one I wanted to answer with a big fat yes? Was it what we were *supposed* to move forward with or just what I *hoped* we could move forward with? I wrestled with these thoughts for a couple of days, praying fervently that my own agenda wouldn't pollute my understanding of what God wanted for our family.

A couple of days later, I felt peace about moving forward with starting our family. My heart softened into more of a "why not?" attitude. And then my prayer shifted from, "God, if this is what we are supposed to do, please show me" to "God, if this is really what we are supposed to do, please put the same prompting in Josh's heart."

Those prayers stayed quietly tucked inside my own heart, and I had every intention of keeping them there until the end of the week. Instead Josh approached me on Wednesday evening. I was standing in our tiny closet of a laundry room, shoving a load of darks into the washer with one hand and holding a bottle of fabric softener in the other.

"Have you thought any more about the baby thing?" he asked me.

"Yes. Have you?" I tried to be casual, but my insides were bursting.

"And … what do you think?" he asked me, his eyebrows raised.

We played chicken for a while, trying to read each other's thoughts, each one not wanting to go first and risking the potential of coloring the opinion of the other. Finally I just begged him to tell me what he was thinking.

"I think we should have a baby!" He grinned from ear to ear.

"Me too!" I let out a big sigh of relief, and we hugged, laughed, and kissed right there in our little laundry room.

I could not believe it. It was astonishing to me how God used postponing Josh's degree program to lead us forward into starting our family.

This story reminds me so much of Proverbs 16:9, "The heart of man plans his way, but the Lord establishes his steps." We can make our own plans certainly. But I think God always wants our hearts to be tender to the changes His sovereign pen makes to the stories we felt sure He was writing for us.

In Christian circles, we often hear the phrase, "When God closes a door, He opens a window!" The phrase has most certainly developed a bit of glibness over the years, what with its frequent usage and all, but I think it does hold a great deal of truth. My father-in-law, Dave, has such a good testimony in this way.

When my Chicago-born father-in-law entered Moody Bible Institute as a college freshman in 1978, he had every intention of studying aviation with what felt to him like a God-given aspiration to become a missionary pilot. He loved the idea of flying missionaries to their various remote locations to spread the gospel.

When Dave began the program, however, it became very obvious very quickly that this was not a place where he would thrive. What he didn't know beforehand—but became very apparent immediately afterward—is that most of the other students in the missionary aviation program already had significant experience operating and flying airplanes. He was under the impression that everyone would start at ground-level zero and work their way up together. Instead it was like joining a group of superstar athletes on the track whom you thought had just started their race but were actually on lap three. There was no real way he could catch up. And so it was with a heart full of disappointment that Dave dropped out of the missionary aviation program. But God still had a wonderful plan in store for him.

Instead of missionary aviation, Dave decided to pursue a ministry degree and spent his days in undergrad with a new dream of becoming a church planter and pastor. Over the last thirty years of his ministry, Dave has led countless souls to a saving knowledge of Jesus Christ. And I know there are untold numbers of others who have been truly changed by him and his gifts as well as his ministry as a pastor, leader, teacher, and shepherd.

It had absolutely not been a part of Dave's plan to be disappointed in this way and forced to give up on his dream of flying as a missionary pilot. But the lives that he has been able to touch in his years as a pastor just prove that God had different plans for how this man's gifts could best be used for the furtherance of His kingdom. My friend Julie has a similar story.

Shortly after they were married, Julie and her husband, Matthew, felt led to pursue foster parenting. The qualifications process for foster parenting is pretty meticulous and notoriously slow, but for Julie and Matthew, it seemed to take even longer than usual. After much deliberation and prayer, they finally decided to put an end to their pursuit of foster parenting and instead began to pursue domestic adoption.

Once again, as time went on, it became clear that domestic adoption was not the path they were supposed to take. Still wanting to be obedient in their call to adoption, Julie and Matthew turned their attention toward international adoption from Ethiopia. In an incredible story of faith and a beautiful picture of God knitting a family together, Julie and her husband were finally able to bring home two boys, biological brothers, to join their forever family.

At the time it seemed so strange to Julie that God very clearly closed the doors to foster parenting and then to domestic adoption. Both of these are such noble and worthy pursuits and most certainly steps of faith that would please the Father who loves nothing more than to see orphans placed in families. But God closed all of those wonderfully worthwhile doors in order to lead Julie's family down the narrow corridor that would bring them to the one door they were meant to open, the one that would introduce them to their two precious sons.

I talked with Julie once about her adoption story. She laughed as she told me that many times people ask her why she and her husband decided to pursue international adoption when the need for domestic adoption is so great.

"We tried!" she said, chuckling. "And God wouldn't let us!"

Sometimes God doesn't allow us to follow through with even very good plans because He has something better in mind. Unfortunately for our hearts prone to wander, it is often only hindsight that can provide us with that perspective. In the meantime, until we gain that perspective that comes only from looking over our shoulders to what God has already done, we can trust the God who knows our hearts and has written every detail of our stories to bring to pass the exact details that best fit into that epic narrative.

Sometimes God places incredibly unexpected turns in the paths of our lives to bring us to the exact place where He wants us to be, for the betterment of our own lives and character and ultimately for the betterment of His kingdom. We can trust the unexpected plot twists in our lives because we know the One writing the script. And we can trust that His sovereign plan is the one that will yield the most fruit in our lives here on earth and the greatest joy in eternity.

The plot twist God wrote into my story in 2010 was a welcome one and the sweetest one I could have imagined. Micah David was born one Sunday afternoon in December, six days before Christmas, after a hard twenty-hour labor. Right after Micah was born, the midwife placed him on my chest. He was crying those big newborn cries from freshly birthed lungs.

I soothed him with gently hushed words. "It's okay, baby. Mama's here." It felt so strange and, at the same time, like such a deep privilege to be someone's mama.

Micah was everything I had wanted, and I absolutely could not believe he was mine. What a sweet gift the Lord gave me at a time when I was not expecting to receive such a treasure. It was a gift I did nothing to deserve, but a very generous and very good gift that God the Father chose to give to His beloved daughter.

God took the plan Josh and I had so carefully constructed and chose instead to give us the gift of a child out of order from what we thought was best. I am incredibly thankful that we were sensitive to the Lord's promptings instead of allowing that closed door to be a stumbling block in our way. We might have been robbed of the sweet blessing of our firstborn at that time had that been the case.

Looking over my shoulder from where I stand today, I see that God had great purpose in allowing that unexpected turn into my life. As I would soon see, having that little boy in my life would be a much-needed bright spot during my darkest season. The whole story of how God led us to begin our family would prove to be a great mercy of the Lord and tangible evidence that I could cling to less than two years later, when pain made it difficult to grasp the truth of God's goodness and sovereignty over my own life.

Broken

Sometimes in life, our plans for ourselves do not go as we had envisioned, and we can become bitter toward God or lose ourselves in striving to bring those plans to fruition.

Beautiful

If we realize that God is the One who writes the plans for our lives, then we can trust that even closed doors are His mercies leading us down the very best path He has always intended for us.

4

PREPARE YOUR HEART FOR THINGS TO COME

It's easy to say that [God's] plans are your most
essential endeavors. It's entirely another thing to live
like it, to participate with Him even when what He's
inviting you to is something you don't understand and
may never have chosen. One person's interruption is
another's divine intervention. One person's problem
is another person's privilege. Which kind of person
do you want to be?[1]

—Priscilla Shirer

Becoming a mother to my precious son was truly my dream come
true, but it was not without challenges. Somewhere in the midst of
wondering how on earth I would ever feel "caught up" with life again
and fretting over whether or not I was equipping my tiny son for a
successful life, I felt the need to stop going to the young families'
Sunday school class at church with my husband and start attending
the ladies-only Sunday school class by myself.

At that time, I really felt like I needed something that was my own.

I craved the company of older, wiser women so I could learn what it meant to be a good mother. I also sought camaraderie and the assurance that motherhood was not only worry, exasperation, and dino-shaped chicken nuggets, but a place where one could grow and even thrive.

In that class, we worked through a Bible study written by Elizabeth George entitled *Loving God with All Your Mind*. Working through that study, I learned truths about God's Word that were absolutely groundbreaking for me: truths on how to tame worries and live in the present, truths on taking every thought captive for Christ, and truths on running the race of life well. But probably the most life-changing truth for me came from the week focused on studying Jeremiah 29:11.

This verse comes in the context of God's instruction to the Israelites after they were captured by the Babylonians and told by God that they would be held captive in that land for the next seventy years. While I imagine every instinct they had at that time would have been much like mine—to freak out, become bitter, worry about everything, and definitely, definitely live like it was not my home—God instructed them otherwise. He told the Israelites, "Build houses and live in them; plant gardens and eat their produce. Take wives and have sons and daughters; take wives for your sons, and give your daughters in marriage, that they may bear sons and daughters; multiply there, and do not decrease."[2]

After the Lord instructs the Israelites on how to live well in the land of their captivity, He tells them to take heart because at the end of those seventy years, they will return to the Promised Land. He assures His people with these ancient words, "'For I know the plans I have for you,' declares the Lord, 'plans to prosper you and not to harm you, to give you a future and a hope.'"[3]

As I studied that verse that particular week, one section of the workbook prompted personal reflection with these questions.

> *What difficult circumstance are you enduring now (or have you endured most recently)? Have you acknowledged God's hand in it? How will doing this help you? It's said that what you think about God will affect your perspective when problems come your way. What kinds*

of thoughts would a faulty and negative view of God produce?[A]

I hesitated to write anything down. Honestly I had nothing great to put there. Sure, there had been some drama in my younger adult years. There had been ups and downs with interpersonal relationships, as there often are in life. But at that time, I could not think of anything big to write down that would allow me to reflect positively on how God used a very difficult circumstance to shape my life for the better or to give me a greater understanding of His character. What I wrote instead was this:

> *God, I can't think of anything to write here. My life has been pretty good. But I realize that something must be coming. And when it does, please help me to react well and handle everything in a way that would be pleasing to You.*

The moment did not feel ominous by any means. But the question was highlighted in my mind. It felt like a truth and a moment in my life that needed to be dog-eared, the corner of the page creased down so I could reference it again. Notably, that was not the only occurrence of a moment like that the year before everything changed.

A few months prior to starting the Elizabeth George study, I read the book, *Hinds' Feet in High Places* by Hannah Hurnard. It is an allegorical story centered on the main character, a young woman with a limp named Much-Afraid and her journey led by the Good Shepherd away from her home in the Valley of Humiliation toward the High Places on the way to the Kingdom of Love. Reading through that book gave me such a new perspective on suffering and hard things and how God can use those difficulties for good to shape our character into exactly the beautiful person He wants us to be.

In one section of the book, Much-Afraid cries out in fear to the Good Shepherd along her journey to the High Places. He answers her kindly.

"Much-Afraid," said the Shepherd again, "tell me, what is the matter. Why were you so fearful?"

"It is the way you have chosen for me to go," she whispered. "It looks so dreadful, Shepherd, so impossible. I turn giddy and faint whenever I look at it. The roes and hinds can go there, but they are not limping, crippled, or cowardly like me."

"But, Much-Afraid, what did I promise you in the Valley of Humiliation?" Asked the Shepherd with a smile.

Much-Afraid looked startled, and the blood rushed into her cheeks and ebbed again, leaving them as white as before. "You said," she began and broke off and then began again. "O Shepherd, you said you would make my feet like hinds' feet and set me upon mine High Places."

"Well," he answered cheerily, "the only way to develop hinds' feet is to go by the paths which the hinds use—like this one."

Much-Afraid trembled and looked at him shamefacedly. "I don't think—I want—hinds' feet, if it means I have to go on a path like that," she said slowly and painfully.

The Shepherd was a very surprising person. Instead of looking either disappointed or disapproving, he actually laughed again.

"Oh, yes you do," he said cheerfully. "I know you better than you know yourself, Much-Afraid. You want it very much indeed, and I promised you these hinds' feet. Indeed, I have brought you on purpose to the back side of the desert, where the mountains are particularly steep and where there are no paths but the tracks of the deer and of the mountain goats for you to follow, that the promise may be fulfilled."[5]

How kind of the Lord to allow me to read such a beautiful story that so perfectly mirrored the suffering I would endure just one year later. I look back in my life at the power of those two pieces of literature—the Bible study and the book—and marvel at a God who knows me intimately. He knows my type-A heart and how much I love to be prepared. I am in awe of these tender gifts from my good Father who was carrying me long before I knew what I needed to be carried for. And the truth-building did not stop there.

Every three years, my father-in-law's church cycles between three main focuses: prayer, neighborhood outreach, and scripture reading. Since 2012 was the year for scripture reading, I committed to reading through the Bible that year. I was quite proud of myself for making it through the "I quit" books of Leviticus and Numbers. When I finally reached the book of Deuteronomy, I buckled down for another chapter of outdated rules, genealogies with real crazy names, and even more specifics on the details of ancient temple artifacts.

What I did not expect, however, was a chapter filled with truth after truth about a God who loves His people deeply and possesses immeasurable, infallible, and omnipotent power. The book of Deuteronomy was holy ground for me. It was oxygen and life. It was God like I had never felt Him before flowing through my veins.

Deuteronomy contains the final words of Moses, the final words he chose to deliver to his people before God took him home to glory. And reading over those words, every last one of them hit me with the same power and passion with which I imagine Moses delivered them to the Israelites.

Every morning I opened up my Bible and my journal and lapped up God's Word like a thirsty puppy, the scribblings in my journal just as fervently messy. I had no idea an Old Testament book could be filled with such life-changing truth about the character of God, and I marveled at how the God of the Ancient Israelites was the same for me as well.

I would read verses like Deuteronomy 7:6, "For you are a holy people to the Lord your God; the Lord your God has chosen you to be a people for Himself, a special treasure above all the peoples on the face of the earth" (New King James Version) and then instantly be reminded of a similar verse in the New Testament, like 1 Peter 2:9, "But you are a chosen generation, a royal priesthood, a holy nation, His own special people, that you may proclaim the praises of Him who called you out of darkness into His marvelous light" (NKJV).

The connections and parallels fascinated me. For well near an hour almost every morning, this was my pattern: dive into deep waters with the Lord and come up gasping at the wonder of His truth, His love, and His character.

It is worth noting that at this time, Micah was around one year old. It is absolutely not lost on me that this tiny boy would keep himself entertained with his books, toys, and copious episodes of *Curious George*. That little guy would stay right next to me in the living room as my sponge-heart soaked up God's Word. I was desperate for it. God made me desperate for it. And He equipped even my sweet toddler son to allow time and space for that to happen.

Popular author, speaker, and host of the *Happy Hour* podcast, Jamie Ivey, often says, "You've either just gone through something hard, are in the middle of something hard, or get ready because something hard is about to happen!" I echo this sentiment, not in an overcast, pessimistic way, but rather as an exhortation to always maintain a state of battle preparation.

The book of James talks about how the trials we face will reveal our hearts and our commitment to the Lord. "Count it all joy, brothers, when you meet trials of various kinds, for you know that the testing of your faith produces steadfastness" (James 1:2).

I've heard it said that when the cup of our hearts is shaken, whatever is inside that cup will spill out. If that is true, then we should intentionally fill our cups with every good and solid truth about this life and the God who gives it to us. That way, when our cups are invariably shaken by the hands of a world steeped in brokenness, what spills out is life water to everyone thirsty for it, even our own parched throats.

While it is never too late to decide to endure life's trials in a way that would best glorify the Father, it is even better to be in a continuous state of heart preparation for when those moments come. If our military decided to train their troops only once a threat was imminent, we would be in sorely bad shape. Instead the military leaders are constantly drilling, practicing, and making dry runs with their equipment. They are always in a state of battle readiness training so that when trouble comes, they will not be caught off guard. So it should be with our hearts.

We should view everything we learn about God and the power of the gospel through the lens of a world tainted by sin and death, with full realization that there is an enemy who seeks to destroy us. When God's Word is spoken into us and over us, we should hide it away in our hearts so we are always ready to use those truths as weapons against darkness.

This life is not easy. Jesus told us—no, assured us—in John 16:33 that we would face difficult times. We can be encouraged that the truth of the gospel allows for hope in these seasons of difficulty because Christ has already overcome death. But we can also be encouraged that God's Word equips us with everything we need to fight and endure. God promises that when we face trying times, He will not leave us or forsake us, and I have come to believe that allowing the truth of His Word to penetrate our hearts is one way that promise will hold true. And it is often that knowledge that becomes the difference between finding the courage to stand bravely and face what comes our way or succumbing to the fear of what we do not know.

I do not serve a God who promised that if I would just place my trust in Him, my life would be easy, carefree, and (hashtag) blessed. I serve and love a God who promises that, when (*when!*) the black storm clouds of life roll in, He will be there to carry me and to give me hope. And I have infinite praise for the God who showed me such tender mercies in preparing my ever-loving, must-have-a-plan heart before ushering me to the front lines, with full and enlightened knowledge of my access to an unlimited, everlasting arsenal of truth.

But sometimes even the bravest and best-prepared soldiers grow weary in the heat of the bloodiest battles.

Broken

Trials and tribulations are an inevitable part of this life on earth.

Beautiful

God's Word is full of every truth we will need to face these trials and tribulations, and He promises to be faithful and carry us through.

PART II

THE END OF THE WORLD AS I KNEW IT

5

IF GOD IS DOING THIS TO ME

You are good and what You do is good …
—Psalm 119:68

The morning of July 16, 2012, I sat in the waiting room of my OB's office, palms under my thighs, swinging my legs with excitement. I may have looked juvenile, but I totally didn't care. The little-kid-on-Christmas-morning feeling was bubbling in my insides as Josh and I anticipated finding out the gender of the little life that had just started to create a noticeable bulge in my middle.

Since we already had a sweet toddler son, I was secretly wishing for a daughter, while outwardly saying the obligatory, "Oh, I don't really care as long as it's healthy!" But I really, *really* wanted a daughter. This feeling was only exacerbated by the recent explosion of Pinterest popularity and the myriad of girly headband ideas that were now at my DIY disposal. I was lost in a daydream of pink-and-white tulle bows and lacy headbands when they called my name.

Inside the dimly lit ultrasound room, I took my place on the small table covered with white crinkly paper. I pulled the top of my waistband down under my tiny twenty-week belly, and the ultrasound technician squirted warm ultrasound gel onto my stomach. I grabbed Josh's hand and squeezed it excitedly. He squeezed back and looked down at me with a twinkle in his eye. We had been here in this same place of excitement and anticipation only two years before. Our hearts were eager to know just a bit more about this new little one who would graduate our family of three to a family of four.

Sue, the ultrasound technician, placed the ultrasound wand on my belly. When she did, the grainy black-and-white image of a tiny human form came onto the flat-screen monitor in front of us.

"Hi, baby," I whispered, smiling to myself.

Two summers before, in that same ultrasound room with the same sonographer, we learned that our Micah would be a bouncing baby boy. I remember so clearly how Sue had positioned her wand, right from the beginning, to give us exactly the news we wanted to hear. Josh and I laughed, and I cried a little, thankful for the little boy we had made together. Then she proceeded with the rest of the ultrasound, measuring arms, legs, belly, head circumference, and on and on to make sure our little boy was growing right on track. This second time around however, the process was noticeably different.

This time, Sue immediately began scanning intently, but not for the telltale gender parts. Instead she scanned around and measured arms and legs, head, and lungs. I was feeling slightly bothered that she was not giving us what we had waited four long months to find out when Sue abruptly asked if we had done a thirteen-week scan, the one typically performed for early detection of developmental abnormalities. I told her no and dismissed this question as incredibly unimportant and wildly annoying. My laser focus on finding out this baby's gender prevented me from seeing the concern in both her eyes and the eyes of my medically literate husband.

The next words out of Sue's mouth were a dream. "It's a little girl …" she began.

"Really?" I asked as tears sprang into the corners of my eyes and slowly dripped down the sides of my face.

Sue nodded yes in response. I stared at the ultrasound screen. A little girl. *A little girl!* The joy began to well up inside of me.

But something in the way Sue's voice trailed off at the end of her sentence kept my excitement from reaching its full potential. It was the ceiling to my helium-filled balloon. Something in the way her voice trailed off led me to believe there was something more that she wasn't telling us. The next words she spoke were the cataclysmic pin-pop to my balloon of rapture.

"Ok, Sarah, I am really concerned about something here," Sue began very matter-of-factly. "I am seeing hardly any amniotic fluid. As far as I can see, the kidneys and stomach look fine, but my machines can't see those details very clearly. We'll need to refer you to a specialist."

My mind went blank. I felt so confused. I felt worried. I even felt a little angry. This was absolutely not how this appointment was supposed to go. And why was she talking about kidneys, stomachs, and things I did not care about? Instead of feeling excited, like I did after Micah's ultrasound, I felt bewildered and unsettled. The light inside of me dimmed.

Josh took my hand and helped me off the bed. We looked at each other with nervous apprehension, both feeling the weight of one thousand questions unpaired with answers. As we prepared to walk out of the room, Sue handed me the prints from the ultrasound images she had just taken.

"I think you'll want to keep these," she said quietly with a somber smile.

I thanked her and took the photos. I wondered why she was acting as if instead of being pregnant with a baby girl, I was carrying a dark omen.

A few hours later, Josh and I were sitting in a small doctor's office, the walls covered with honey-oak paneling. We sat together on one side of the circular table, hardly able to look at each other, but grasping hands tightly, both holding back tears. We were not sure what was happening with our unborn baby girl. But after our experience that morning at the OB's office and especially after hearing the hushed whispers of both high-risk doctors for the last hour in a second ultrasound at the maternal-fetal medicine specialist, we had a pretty good idea that whatever the news was, it would not be good.

The doctor entered his office and smiled weakly as he sat down across the table from us. He slowly spread two pieces of paper in front of us and proceeded to draw two different diagrams, one on each paper.

"Here is what a healthy fetal urinary system should look like," he explained his drawing in a thick Indian accent.

His diagram showed what any fully functioning infant urinary system would look like: healthy kidneys filtering through attached and fully functioning ureters, ureters feeding into an intact bladder, and the bladder collecting the urine that the baby would eventually pass into the amniotic sac, creating the amniotic fluid necessary for the healthy growth of the baby. Besides the little fact about amniotic fluid being comprised of baby urine, this information wasn't anything I hadn't learned in my Human Biology 101 class my freshman year of college.

But then the doctor began to contrast that first diagram with a second one, this one representing a model of our own baby girl's urinary system.

"What we are finding here ..." He drew as he talked. "Is that your baby has many cysts on her kidneys. The ureters are not connected and have even atrophied because they are not in use. The bladder ... we cannot see it. All of this makes it impossible for the baby to pass urine and therefore constricts the baby's growing environment since there is no increase in amniotic fluid."

He then told us that this restricted growth environment causes something called hypoplastic (underdeveloped) lungs. The restricted growth environment would also impede our baby's continued cardiac development, resulting in a very weak heart.

"Babies like this," he continued, keeping his head down but his eyes on both of us, "cannot live on their own outside of the womb."

His words reverberated in my head as every other sound was drowned out by the pounding of my heartbeat in my own ears. The corners of my vision began to darken as I focused my eyes on the two diagrams in front of me.

Babies like this can't live on their own outside of the womb ... babies like this can't live on their own outside of the womb.

I heard the statement. I understood the words. But it took all my mental and physical energy to understand what the words meant for *me*.

If babies like this can't live outside of the womb, then this baby is going to die. If this baby is going to die, that means I will spend the rest of my pregnancy with a baby who will not come home with us.

Our baby will not come home with us.

The tears began to fall on their own, but I held them back. I would soon become a master at holding them back. I was desperate for this not to be my reality.

"What is the survival rate for babies like this?" I choked out, my eyes begging the doctor for even a thimbleful of good news.

"The survival rate is only about five percent," the doctor reported back to me.

I felt a little spring of hope well up inside of me. "Then we'll fight for that five percent! What ... What can we do?" My question was desperate. I wanted anything that would prevent the tried-and-true medical odds from becoming my reality.

Josh gently put his hand on my leg. "Sarah, a five percent survival rate basically means there is no chance of survival. There's nothing ..." his voice trailed off. He looked away, tears pooling in his Daddy eyes.

My desperate eyes darted back and forth between my husband and the doctor. I was in shock. Throughout the entire day, I had been preparing myself for the possibilities of this obviously troubled pregnancy. I imagined that we might have a child with special needs who would require expert medical care. I imagined myself on bed rest, maybe a premature birth, possibly weeks in the NICU for our sweet baby. But never, ever did I envision a future where the end of whatever long trial we had to endure would bring us home from a birthing experience, arms empty.

The doctor asked us if we had any questions, offered his condolences, and then gently sent us on our way. He reassured me that I was in good hands with him and his high-risk obstetric team. I nodded a tearful thank you, my mind still hazy from the shock and heaviness of it all.

Josh and I exited the doctor's office and entered the elevator lobby. I quickly walked ahead of him, stumbling under the weight of my very overwhelming and disorienting reality. My insides were shaking, tears were stinging in my eyes, and the scream in my throat violently threatened to break free. I repeatedly pushed the elevator button, as if each press could make the elevator appear that much faster and possibly even whisk me away from my actuality.

As I stood in front of the stainless-steel doors, willing for them to open, Josh grabbed me by the shoulders and swung me around, pulling me deep into his heaving chest. I buried my face into his shirt, and we clung tightly to each other, wishing each one of us could take away the other's pain. We stood there and wailed loud, mourning tears, as only two parents facing the death of a child possibly could. Our baby girl was going to die. What else was there to do but weep?

We drove back home in relative silence, save for a few moments of mumbling over what to do for dinner. Neither one of us felt hungry.

As we drove home that humid summer evening, I stared out the window and tried to imagine what my life would look like for the next several months as we anticipated the death of our unborn baby girl. I also tried to imagine how a good God could let something so awful happen to two of His beloved children. But somewhere in the midst of my questions and attempts to make sense of the myriad of unknowns, the Lord brought to mind a quote from George Müller that I had heard several months before. *If God is doing this to me, it must be the best thing for me.*

George Müller was an amazing man of God who spent his life caring for and educating orphans in England in the mid-nineteenth century. George Müller established well over 100 schools and educated over 120,000 children during his ministry. He was a man of great faith. As George Müller's wife, Mary, lay dying of cancer and as he watched the life of his beloved slowly fade away, this giant of the faith whispered those great words, "If God is doing this to me, it must be the best thing for me."[1]

I heard that powerful quote one Sunday morning as my father-in-law shared it from the pulpit. Honestly, the level of faith displayed in that statement took my breath away. I could absolutely not imagine going through something as painful as the death of your spouse and holding such an incredibly humble, surrendered heart posture to call it God's best. The story behind that quote made such a lasting impression on me as a beautiful example of surrender to God's perfect will, even in a season of deep loss and heartache.

But now it was my turn. It was my turn to look at my life and the circumstances where death seemed to have the upper hand and determine how this could be God's best in my own life. Undeniably, any halfway decent individual on this earth would label a fatal diagnosis of an unborn baby as bad or hard or even impossible. How could this situation possibly be God's *best* for me? The Old Testament story of Joseph holds some incredible insights when considering God's best in our own lives.

Genesis 27 begins Joseph's story. You might be familiar with the story, how Joseph was his father's favorite son but the most hated among his brothers. After Joseph interpreted a series of dreams to his brothers that meant one day they would bow down to him, the brothers had the last straw and threw Joseph into a pit, intending to return later and kill him. Instead they sold him to slave traders and concocted an elaborate story for their father of how Joseph had been mauled to death by a wild animal.

The slave traders took Joseph to Egypt, and he was sold to a wealthy man named Potiphar. Although he was a slave, Joseph earned favorable status with Potiphar and became his most trusted estate manager. When Potiphar's wife attempted to seduce Joseph and he declined her invitation, I imagine it was her sense of rejection and embarrassment that compelled her to falsely accuse Joseph of rape.

Joseph spent some time in prison, and while he was there, the Lord gave him the ability to interpret dreams. He accurately interpreted dreams for two men who said they would remember Joseph once they were freed, but they forgot him. Despite their forgetfulness, Joseph's gift of dream interpretation soon earned him a reputation so great that it attracted the attention of Pharaoh himself. When Joseph correctly interpreted the leader's dreams and led Pharaoh to enact a plan that would save the Egyptian people from famine, Joseph was promoted to a position of highest honor.

Indeed, just as Joseph had predicted, the land of Egypt and the surrounding areas were soon plagued by a great famine. But since Joseph had forewarned the king, Egypt had stockpiled several years' worth of grain and other supplies into their storehouses. Before long, the surrounding people groups traveled to Egypt for food, a group that included Joseph's people, the Israelites, and the brothers who had so heartlessly betrayed him.

In Genesis 50, Joseph's brothers bow before him in deep remorse over the way they had treated him so many years before. They also fear the revenge their powerful brother could exact upon them. But Joseph's gentle words of kindness and forgiveness reverberate in my heart as one who has doubted the Lord's ways too many times to count. "What you meant for evil, God meant for good, to save much people alive" (Genesis 50:20).

I think I would consider a large portion of Joseph's story bad. He was thrown into a pit, sold into slavery, wrongfully accused, imprisoned, and forgotten. Not one of those things are inherently good. So many parts of Joseph's story could be considered bad.

But as we look at the pinnacle of why he was brought to Egypt, we can so clearly see how those bad things led him to a place where he could do so much good, where he had the ability to save a great many people, including the whole of the nation of Israel.

Could the same be true in our lives as well? Could the very situations that we deem to be too difficult really be meant to put us on a path for the ultimate good of ourselves and God's forever kingdom?

Author and pastor Max Lucado tells a fictional narrative about an old woodcutter. This tale perfectly illustrates this idea that we do not really have capabilities to distinguish what is good and what is bad with respect to our own stories because we do not know the end of the story.

> Once there was an old man who lived in a tiny village. Although poor, he was envied by all, for he owned a beautiful white horse. One morning he found that

the horse was not in the stable. All the village came to see him.

"You old fool," they scoffed, "we told you that someone would steal your horse. We warned you that you would be robbed. You are so poor. How could you ever hope to protect such a valuable animal? It would have been better to have sold him. Now the horse is gone, and you've been cursed with misfortune."

The old man spoke. "All I know is that the stable is empty, and the horse is gone. The rest I don't know. Whether it be a curse or a blessing, I can't say. All we can see is a fragment. Who can say what will come next?"

After fifteen days, the horse returned. He hadn't been stolen; he had run away into the forest. Not only had he returned, he had brought a dozen wild horses with him. Once again the village people gathered around the woodcutter and spoke.

"Old man, you were right and we were wrong. What we thought was a curse was a blessing. Please forgive us."

The man responded, "Once again, you go too far. Say only that the horse is back. State only that a dozen horses returned with him, but don't judge. How do you know if this is a blessing or not? You see only a fragment. Unless you know the whole story, how can you judge? You read only one page of a book. Can you judge the whole book? You read only one word of a phrase. Can you understand the entire phrase?"[2]

At any given point in time, we only know a small portion of our story, a singular scope of the complete panoramic view. Because we don't know the end of our own stories, we cannot possibly have the foresight to say whether or not a thing is good or bad, detrimental, or God's best. And as stories like Joseph's show us, sometimes the hardest, most difficult things can lead to the salvation of many, even our own souls.

That day, driving home from that fateful doctor's appointment, I hardly knew what it meant: *this is the best thing for me.* How could this situation that would ultimately lead to the death of an infant be the best thing for me?

But sometimes in those places where we find ourselves at the end of what makes sense, the only thing that begins to make sense is to let go of our own understanding and reach out to the only One who truly knows, the One who can work good from all things … even this.

Broken

Bad things happen to even very good, nice, well-meaning people who follow Jesus.

Beautiful

God is writing a story for each one of us. Even the most painful things in our lives can be used for good because they come from a God who can only do good and who will work it all for the ultimate good of His kingdom.

6

ALL OF ME

The first and foremost thing we can conclude with
certainty about a child is this: Every child conceived
is a God-created and God-loved person with a God-
given purpose and destiny. Let your comfort begin
with that truth.[1]

—John MacArthur

The night our baby girl was diagnosed, I lingered longer than usual
in Micah's bedroom after tucking him under his covers. Before bed,
Micah and I read *Curious George Goes to a Baseball Game*, a book
we frequently checked out from the local library. But this night I
struggled to read the familiar story. I choked up at the part of the
story where little boy becomes separated from his daddy. Of course the
story ends on a high note, with George's curiosity and troublemaking
antics vindicated because he reunited the little boy with his father. It is
a sweet, albeit predictable ending, as most Curious George books are.
How I wished in that moment for my life to be as sweet and predictable
as a Curious George story.

As Micah slept soundly in his crib, I sat in the glider in the corner
of his room, my hands resting on my twenty-week belly. In the quiet

and in the stillness, my heart tried so hard to make sense of what to feel about this broken little girl growing inside of me. I had no trouble loving Micah. He was adorable, sweet, and easy to be around. I loved seeing the world through his eyes and teaching him about caterpillars and clouds and how to pump his legs on the swing. It was not hard to love him and enjoy our beautiful, reciprocal, affectionate relationship. This was motherly love as I knew it. But my maternal heart struggled to know how to love this baby girl whose existence would be tumultuous, emotionally draining, and agonizingly brief.

I knew what the doctors felt about her. She was expendable. We had been offered the option to terminate, to end it all right then and there. We denied this option, knowing that terminating the pregnancy would likely only compound our grief rather than alleviate it. Still though, in that moment, feeling all the fear of every unknown in an impossible situation like the one we were in, a very distinct thought ran across my mind, clear and undeniable. *This is why people choose this. This is why …*

My friend Mary-Evelyn Smith wrote a beautiful reflection about the moment doctors offered to terminate her pregnancy after her unborn son was diagnosed with spina bifida.

> Terminate. The word fell at my feet. Not with the hard thud of a hammer or the fearsome crash of a shattered dish. No. It dropped like the soft plunk of an apple falling on grass. Like something sweet and round, delicious and cool. Like something I wanted so badly to eat.

> Up until then, I had never understood. Up until then, abortion was an "issue." But all that changed when it landed at my feet, an escape plan lying just within my reach. For a moment, I wanted it. Not because I am a monster, not because I don't love my child, and not because I had changed my stance on the issue. I

wanted to do it because I was terrified and because everything around me was collapsing.

If you thought you were in a burning building, you'd find the nearest exit too.[2]

Like Mary Evelyn, we chose not to terminate. We believe life is sacred and a gift from God. Truthfully though, it is so much harder to believe in the sacredness of life when that life brings with it an unwelcome load of heartache and pain, of confusion and uncertainty.

Scripture tells us that all life is important to God and that every person is worth Christ's shed blood. But what about this little life? What about this little girl whose body was so broken that her lungs would fail her once she was outside of the womb? God's Word is clear that children are a blessing, a joy, a crown of pride for their parents. But what about this one?

Psalm 139:13–14 holds this beautiful truth. "For you formed my inward parts; you knitted me together in my mother's womb. I praise you, for I am fearfully and wonderfully made. Wonderful are your works; my soul knows it very well."

God formed the parts of this little baby girl. He formed every single part, even the ones that were underdeveloped or absent. He formed them just as He wanted to. And He called them beautiful, wonderful, specially made, and marvelous, just the way He wanted them to be.

A few verses down in the same psalm, these truths continue. "My frame was not hidden from you, when I was made in secret, intricately woven in the depths of the earth. You saw my unformed substance; in your book were written, every one of them, the days that were formed for me, when as yet there were none of them."[3]

Those sacred, ancient words communicate the truth that my broken baby was made this way on purpose—for a purpose—by the One who gives meaning and purpose to all things. He formed her parts, however broken, and wrote her days, however short, into the beautiful story He penned for the universe.

My pregnancy—her life—could have been terminated with almost no consequence or second thought. Some may not even have considered it a loss. But not to God. Not to the Creator of all things. And while I don't pretend to know why He wanted my baby girl to be formed in this unquestionably imperfect way, this is precisely how He wanted her to be and exactly how He called her beautiful and beloved.

While these verses brought a great deal of comfort to my freshly breaking heart, knowing how deeply God loved and valued my daughter despite her brokenness, it was quite another thing to bring myself to feel the same depth of love. It was so difficult to think about and embrace the value of this baby's life. What value could I place on this little person who had turned my world upside down and whose untimely absence would undoubtedly shatter my heart?

My instinct was self-preservation. I strategized how I could possibly carry this baby without becoming attached and thereby minimize, or possibly even bypass, the depth of loss I would feel once she passed away.

Singer-songwriter Matt Hammitt of the band Sanctus Real and his wife, Sarah, were told during a routine ultrasound that their unborn son, Bowen, had a severe heart defect called hypoplastic left heart syndrome (HLHS). This condition meant that the left side of Bowen's heart was severely underdeveloped. Matt and Sarah were pressed face-to-face with the reality that their son might not live very long after birth.

Babies with HLHS need surgery just to survive. The trouble is that sometimes these life-saving surgeries can become life-claiming surgeries. The surgeries are intrusive and risky and must be performed on the bodies of these already fragile newborns.

In an effort to protect himself from the potential of devastating heartache, Matt closed himself off from bonding with his unborn son. Matt was so deeply afraid that Bowen's broken heart would break his own. But after some time, Matt realized he needed to love his fragile son with the same reckless abandon with which God loves us. Out of this realization came a beautiful lullaby for baby Bowen.

You're gonna have all of me

You're gonna have all of me
'Cause you're worth every falling tear
You're worth facing any fear
You're gonna know all my love
Even if it's not enough
Enough to mend our broken hearts
But giving you all of me is where I'll start.[4]

As I sat in the rocking chair that night, the Lord brought the lyrics of that beautiful song to mind. Even more significantly though, the Lord brought to mind the story behind the song, a story I had heard just a few months prior on the local Christian radio station. In that moment of searching my own heart, the story of Matt and baby Bowen met me and moved me toward a deeper understanding of how I was supposed to feel about my tiny baby girl.

When we love, we risk being broken. When we love, we give a vulnerable part of ourselves to another without any assurance of how they will treat our love or our hearts. But God did the same for us when He created us. And He did the same when Jesus gave His life to pay the price for our sins, the ultimate expression of love. And while we can never fully sacrifice to the extent that Jesus did when He washed our sins with His own blood, we are called to live and love as Christ does, even if just a silhouette's worth. And we are all the better for it.

As Ann Voskamp writes in her book *The Broken Way*, "Love pries open your chest and pulls open the door of your heart so someone can walk right in and make this mess that makes you into something more beautiful."[5]

Jessica Paulraj has her own story of how God called her to love in this same beautifully messy way. Jessica and her husband, Raja, felt led to add to their family through the blessing of adoption. More specifically, they felt led to adopt Adam, a little boy with life-threatening special needs. The doctors and nurses in the hospital where Adam lived told Jessica and her husband that this little boy was dying and that palliative care was the only option for him.

As Jessica prayed through the challenge of adopting this fragile little boy, she wrestled with what it would look like to adopt a child with a very limited number of days, a child whom she would inevitably outlive. She reflected on the mental process God led her through while wrestling with this decision and beautifully shared her thoughts in a blog post.

> Can I raise a dying child? Again and again this question consumed me. Can I love him as my own and treasure each moment knowing he is dying?
>
> I imagined so much pain. I feared not having joy or time. But God's still small voice echoed in the darkness of the deep confines of my heart and mind: *Jessica, my daughter, you too, are dying. Raja, your beloved husband, he too is dying.*
>
> Yes, our Spirits will live. But this body, it is fading. After all, didn't Solomon tell us, "There is a time for everything, and a season for every activity under heaven, a time to be born and a time to die ...?" For, "All men are like grass, and all their glory is like the flowers of the field; the grass withers and the flowers fall, but the Word of the Lord stands forever."
>
> Yes, we are eternal beings. That I know. And in that I rejoice. We will one day see all things made new! The idea that we are all dying is not fatalistic. It is Truth. Each year that passes, I see changes in my own body. We age and no man knows if he is guaranteed tomorrow
>
> Again, in my spirit, He asked, "Did you choose to not marry Raja because one day he may die before you?"
>
> No.

"Do you love him or any of your family and friends less because of unavoidable death?"

No.

I love them deeply in this moment. Then why should I question loving, adopting, and caring for this precious boy because medicine says he will have a shortened life?[5]

Just as Jessica and her husband and Matt and his wife were called to love their broken baby boys, loving fully and giving all of myself, recklessly even, to this baby girl was my calling. God very intentionally wove our stories together: me a part of hers and hers forever a part of mine. I had no choice but to give her every ounce of my love, to give myself fully to whom she would be, and to let that shape my heart, even if the shaping meant ripping and tearing, bleeding, and scarring.

Somehow deep down I knew that even if I tried to distance myself from bonding with my baby, the distance would not provide the preservation I had hoped for. My baby girl and I were divinely and inexplicably intertwined by a God who is sovereign, who wrote this story into both of our days and claimed beauty and purpose in both.

In an unfiltered moment of external processing the afternoon after our baby's diagnosis, I blubbered out a question to my mother-in-law, Teresa. "This baby won't even matter! I mean, are we even supposed to give her a name?"

The words may have shocked both of us, but Teresa's voice and eyes were kind, both laced with all the emotion of a grandmother anticipating the loss of her first granddaughter.

"Oh yes," she said quietly, stroking my hair, "you should give her a name."

I nodded weakly, knowingly. I hadn't wanted to give her a name. I hadn't wanted to make her real, to make this a thing. But it was. It had to be. *She* had to be. She was always meant to be.

That night in Micah's room, I stood up slowly from the rocking chair after a good hour of rocking, thinking, and processing and walked down the hallway and out into the living room where Josh sat on the couch. His laptop was open. He was answering dozens of emails, texts, and Facebook messages from concerned and loving friends and family. He looked up at me, eyes weary with tears.

"I want to name her Evie," I said decidedly. "Evie Caris. I want to give her the name we picked out for a girl. I want to use that name."

Josh nodded slowly, his eyes full of understanding. He knew how much that name meant to me. It was my favorite girl name, the one I had hopefully written on napkins and paper scraps as I daydreamed of what our family would look like one day. This was certainly not the story I had dreamed about for our family for so many years. This situation was not how I imagined bringing our first daughter into the world. But the name was meant for her.

Evie means life; Caris means grace. Life and grace. Life for a special girl who would know a short life here but was destined for an eternity in the presence of the Father. Grace for a situation that would require a greater measure than we ever realized could possibly be needed in one lifetime.

Evie Caris. She had stolen my heart.

Broken

The world is filled with broken people, people whose bodies and hearts fail but who still require love. Often this love can feel laborious and push us far outside of our own personal comfort levels.

Beautiful

God has a special story and unique purpose for each person, and we can fully love each one of these people because of the massive love God has for all of us and the sacrificial love shown to us through Jesus Christ.

THE NEXT RIGHT THING

> God's goodness and power are not to be measured in
> the balance of tragedy and adversity we experience day
> in and day out. If His goodness is to be questioned,
> let it be done in light of His original purpose as well
> as His ultimate plan.[1]
>
> —Charles Stanley

The moment we posted the news regarding Evie's poor prognosis on
social media, Josh and I received a gracious outpouring of love from
friends and family. Not only did close friends and family reach out to
encourage us, but friends we had not spoken to for some time contacted
us to tell us they were praying for us and thinking of us and would
continue to do so as we faced the long months ahead. So many also
wrote to us about their own losses and offered Josh and me a listening
ear if we ever needed one. Their kind words brought some level of solace
to my otherwise tumultuous emotions.

I spent an entirety of two days glued to my computer and phone
screens, pouring over every single empathetic word. Secretly, I hoped
that one of the messages would contain some supernatural insight that
would tell me this was all totally unreal and that we would absolutely,

positively, in no circumstance have to say goodbye to our baby girl. But no amount of refreshing my news feed could bring such an assurance.

For two days, my eyes felt fuzzy, and my brain felt hazy from a combination of crying and computer-screen staring. After those two days, I finally decided I could not live like this anymore; I could not spend the next four months of my life hanging onto every red Facebook notification. I had to live, and I had to do life. But how could I move forward when my life, which once felt like stable ground, was now splintered and fragmented like the rotting slats of a creaky rope bridge?

Elisabeth Elliot is revered as one of the most influential Christian women of the modern era. She endeared herself to many through her radio show, *Gateway to Joy*, where she spoke to audiences about the goodness of God, drawing from her experiences as a wife, mother, widow, and missionary. She would always begin her radio segments with this sweet introduction, "You are loved with an everlasting love. And underneath are the everlasting arms."

In 1952, Elisabeth Elliot traveled to Ecuador with her husband, Jim, to follow his vision of reaching the native people with the good news of Jesus Christ. In January 1956, Jim was speared to death by the very people he was trying to serve. This left Elisabeth widowed at age thirty, in a foreign country, and a newly single parent to her ten-month-old daughter, Valerie.

Calling this situation hard would be quite the understatement, like calling Niagara Falls wet or the surface of the sun warm-ish. The depth of mental and emotional turmoil young Elisabeth Elliot was plunged into begs the question of how she survived it all. And it is an honest question.

How on earth did she manage her sanity after her husband's murder? How did she find the strength to raise her daughter, alone? How did she overcome the shock of her husband's death and put one foot in front of the other when her world suddenly became a balancing act upon a narrow wall of crumbling stone? This deeply faith-filled woman of God told us exactly how.

When I went back to my jungle station after the death of my first husband, Jim Elliot, I was faced with many confusions and uncertainties. I had a good many new roles, besides that of being a single parent and a widow. I was alone on a jungle station that Jim and I had manned together. I had to learn to do all kinds of things, which I was not trained or prepared in any way to do. It was a great help to me simply to do the next thing.

Have you had the experience of feeling as if you've got far too many burdens to bear, far too many people to take care of, far too many things on your list to do? You just can't possibly do it, and you get in a panic and you just want to sit down and collapse in a pile and feel sorry for yourself. Well, I've felt that way a good many times in my life, and I go back over and over again to an old Saxon legend, which I'm told is carved in an old English parson somewhere by the sea. The poem says, "Do it immediately, do it with prayer, do it reliantly, casting all care. Do it with reverence, tracing His hand, who placed it before thee with earnest command. Stayed on omnipotence, safe 'neath His wing, leave all resultings, do the next thing."

That is a wonderfully saving truth. Just do the next thing.[2]

Just do the next thing. It is a wonderfully simple concept but can be the difference between allowing difficult circumstances to paralyze us from living or providing hope and purpose when all hope and purpose seem lost.

Just do the next thing. I've even heard this phrase with the addition of one little word: just do the next *right* thing. With the life of these words pulsing through my veins, I felt determined to try to move on with my regular, everyday life after learning of Evie's fatal diagnosis.

As much as possible, I really did not want the next four months to be ruled by the impending loss of my baby girl. I had a house, a toddler son, and a husband who needed my attention, and I wanted to give them the best of me that I possibly could despite the circumstances. So I defaulted back into my familiar routine of housekeeping and spending time with Micah and all the other normalcies that characterized my life before Evie's diagnosis. Truthfully, there was a small bit of comfort in falling back into that predictable routine, considering the unpredictable situation I found myself in otherwise.

Even still, pushing forward with normal life was so very hard, like attempting to swim laps in the pool while wearing cement shoes or being pulled out of a dead sleep to play a round of double-dutch. There was absolutely nothing inside of me that felt like doing anything, let alone a next thing or a right thing. Mostly I wanted to do a sleeping thing or a lying-in-bed-crying thing. Grief is like that. It makes even the most diligent among us heavy with malaise.

In her book *Choosing to See*, Mary Beth Chapman describes a very similar sentiment after losing her daughter Maria to a tragic accident in their own driveway. She describes what it was like coming home and attempting to do the next right thing.

> We put our bags down inside and tried to do normal things, even though the quiet was so loud without Maria giggling and running and bouncing around everywhere. We got some laundry started and put our stuff away. We were mostly focused on [our other daughters], trying to make things as normal for them as we could … as if that were possible.[3]

Although I had not yet lost Evie at that point, it is fair to say that I was already grieving. I was grieving my new reality, the one where the baby we thought would be coming home with us would instead take her first and last breaths inside the same hospital room where she was born.

I was grieving a lifetime of memories we would never get to make. I was grieving the loss of my dream of becoming a mother to this little one, grieving for how my life would change, and grieving for my son and my husband and what this would mean in their lives as well. I grieved the death of the perfectly packaged life I had planned out for myself.

In addition to grieving those losses, there was something else I was grieving deeply, something that I felt needed to be said in hushed tones or maybe not spoken out loud at all. It felt like a thing that was against scripture and against everything that people expected of a good Christian person who claimed to love Jesus. But one part of what made it so hard to move on and put one foot in front of the other—to do the next right thing—was that I felt as though God had let me down.

All my life I had lived well for the Lord as a good example of what a Christian young woman should be. I believed what I thought to be truth: if you obey God's commands and live in a way that pleases Him, your life will be relatively great. Sure, there may be bumps and bruises along the way, but nothing too debilitating.

Part of the struggle of doing the next right thing after Evie's diagnosis was that I now felt like I lived in a world where God was dangerous and likely to yank the rug right out from under what I believed to be my own well-established and sturdy ground. It was so hard to move forward because the world as I had come to understand it was now an avalanche of chaos and I struggled to gain footing.

It is the age-old question of why bad things happen to good people. And if good people serve a good God, then what can we call the thing that happens when lovers of Jesus find themselves deep in the throes of cancer or divorce or the horrors of abuse?

In his book *A Grief Observed*, C. S. Lewis pens his thoughts after the loss of his wife, Joy, to cancer. He struggled with this same question, this question of God maintaining a character of undeniable goodness in the midst of deep sorrow.

> Sooner or later I must face the question in plain language. What reason have we, except our own desperate wishes, to believe that God is, by any

standard we can conceive, "good"? Doesn't all the prima facie evidence suggest exactly the opposite? What have we to set against it?

We set Christ against it.[4]

When we are threatened to feel as though God, in our most desperate hour, has forgotten, forsaken, or betrayed us, it becomes necessary to do as C. S. Lewis said, to set Christ against those feelings. Our God is only good, and when the consequences of the fall threatened to sever us from the Father for eternity, Christ paid our way with crimson currency, His own flesh and blood. When the enemy seeps into our broken hearts as they pulse with the pain of our reality, he whispers untruth with his sinister tongue, lies about how God cannot be trusted, and does not really care. When that happens, may we never forget that God more than cares. He made a way! When all was lost in sin and chaos, God made a way for all of us to be made new through the shed blood of Jesus. O praise Him!

Even still, I do know this truth can be incredibly difficult to face straight on when our hearts are hurting so badly. When our world formerly known as good and safe is suddenly wrecked by something catastrophic, painful, and wildly unsettling, the things we may have thought would bring the most comfort might suddenly feel very off-putting or repulsive even, like the screech of fingers on a balloon. Every well-intentioned word from a friend can feel like criticism and condescension. Every praise song can feel like a taunt. Every scriptural verse we ever knew, quoted, or hid in our hearts might feel like a cruel tool of torment aimed at our weakened spirits.

But the truth is that nothing can change the absolute truth that Jesus Christ came to this earth to die for our sins, defeat death, and now lives so that one day we can join Him in a place where there will be no more sorrow, pain, and tears. May this truth gently nudge us toward the next right thing, even if our feet can only manage to shuffle.

Sometimes the next right thing looks very much like throwing our legs over the side of the bed, planting our feet firmly on the floor, and resolving to stand up, walk to the kitchen, and start a pot of coffee because today is a new day. Sometimes the next right thing looks like giving ourselves the space to cry and to grieve deeply. Sometimes it looks like finally sharing our vulnerable realities to a friend and letting the tears fall. Sometimes it looks like calling to make an appointment to get real, professional help this time. These are steps we can physically take to do the next right thing after tragedy strikes.

But just as we must put one foot in front of the other physically and determine to take actual steps to beat back the darkness, we must also do so spiritually. We must train ourselves to swim upstream, against what grief, loss, and painful circumstances make us *feel*—that God is bad and unable to be trusted—and fix our eyes instead on what we knew to be fact, to be undeniably true before the unthinkable happened: that God is good and capable of only good, that He is truth and love and abounding in mercy, that His love endures forever, and that Jesus defeated death and made a way for us to defy it as well. As the band Rend Collective sings, "What is true in the light is still true in the dark."[5]

The next right thing is always, always to feed ourselves truth. God's Word and His truths are solid and stable even when we are not. God may feel distant or cruel, but His Word reveals a different God than we feel. God's Word reveals One whose words are capable of sustaining through difficult times and who intends to carry us through it all by the power of His never-ending grace.

Broken

Painful circumstances can send us in a hazy fog that threaten to paralyze us both physically and spiritually.

Beautiful

The truth of God's Word can lead us to do the next right thing, which includes leaning hard on the truth of His character so darkness will not defeat both our bodies and our souls.

THE WAITING MONTHS

> The Bible is shockingly honest. And because of that,
> I can be honest as well. I can both complain and cry,
> knowing that God can handle anything I say. The
> Lord wants me to talk to Him, to pour out my heart
> and my thoughts unedited because He knows them
> already.[1]
>
> —Vaneetha Rendall Risner

Life, for the most part, consists of particular circumstances paired
with predictable outcomes. Thanksgiving means roasted turkey,
and Christmas always means gifts. A wedding usually follows an
engagement, a graduation ceremony typically follows four years of
college, and babies are born and then brought home to thoughtfully
and tenderly decorated nurseries. Our expectation of the typical flow
of life follows generations of confirmation and generations of relative
predictability.

But if you stand back and observe life with fresh eyes, you might
find all around you a random sample of individuals whose lives do not
follow that expectant predictability. Engagements are broken. College
is not for everyone. Sometimes the holiday budget that year does not

allow a margin for gifts or maybe not even for a whole turkey. And sometimes, mommies grow babies in their bellies, and those babies never get to come home.

I found myself there, living every day in the place where what I had always expected to happen was crushed under the weight of tragedy. Pregnancy and birth no longer equated a lifetime of tenderly caring for a little soul. Instead pregnancy and the subsequent birth became a twisted amalgamation of fear and sadness, of anticipating goodbye. It felt impossible.

Josh and I were so happy when we found out we were pregnant for the second time. We told our friends and family at my mother-in-law's surprise fiftieth birthday party. In her birthday card, I had written, "Happy birthday, Mamma. We love you, love Daddy, Mommy, Micah, and Baby #2!" There were big smiles and even bigger hugs as friends and family congratulated us on our special news. The moment had been perfect.

This baby was so loved, so wanted, and so celebrated. On that happy reveal day, we could never have predicted that this little bundle of joy would spend her short life in the hospital and that most of the loved ones who celebrated with us would never even get to hold her or kiss her sweet face.

I spent the days, weeks, and months of my pregnancy with Evie in a sort of alternate, surreal reality. It was as if I had been traveling down life's path on my own merry way, blissfully expecting all the normalcy of a young family. Then suddenly my course was drastically changed, a road closed, the life-map GPS in my brain suddenly forced to recalculate a surrogate route. And the majority of every day was spent trying to figure out how to navigate within that abrupt and unwelcome recalculation.

So many things during those months carrying Evie after her diagnosis felt immensely confusing. I was a stranger in my own body and in my own mind. I was exhausted from the constant tears and from trying to maintain any semblance of normalcy.

It was tiring, trying to live this strange life wherein everything on the outside appeared very normal and happy, the proverbial American dream. But inside my mind was bedlam, my heart was scraped raw, and our baby girl was not well. It took every shred of strength from the most microscopic edges of my cellular composition to keep my mind focused on God's truth and His promise of provision during hard times so the enemy would not overtake my soul. Heaven knows he tried.

My emotional state was fragile and lacked the structural integrity it had once known so well, like a cardboard box beaten down by the rain. This was deeply unsettling to me. If God were my strength, if He were indeed carrying me through the fire as He promised, then why did I feel so weak and so vulnerable? Why did I have to work so hard to find hope, joy, and peace? Where was the peace that passes all understanding, and why was it not flooding over me and washing away my anguish? Why, if I were a child of the Father of light, did I have to fight so hard to see that light?

One evening I was really upset by how all of this felt. I was convinced that I was somehow doing this whole suffering thing wrong. My mind equated peace with absolute resolve. My mind equated peace with having a heart of Kevlar, unfazed by bullets or the stab of a blade. In my mind, the peace and strength from the Holy Spirit and the comfort of the truth of the Father would cancel out any and all fears, doubts, and questions about what was happening in my life right then. I was certain that if I were really doing this right and in a way that would bring glory to the Father, I would feel much differently.

I called my father-in-law, Dave, and tearfully poured out all of these concerns to him over the phone. I explained that I did not know why on earth it felt so hard to keep my mind in a good place and to keep my eyes focused on Jesus. I asked him why this was so hard. Was it supposed to be this hard?

His words were tender and kind, soothing and understanding. He told me that what I was going through was indeed immensely hard. He used an example of a woman who had endured all the horrors of a German concentration camp, a Holocaust survivor who said that, in many ways, dealing with the rejection of divorce from her husband many years later was even more painful than what she had experienced in the concentration camp. What I was going through would maybe even be considered hard by the most seasoned of sufferers.

I asked Dave why I did not simply feel the peace and the joy that I thought was promised in scripture, why it wasn't washing over me and washing away any fears or concerns. He kindly told me that peace and joy are a choice and something we must fight for. Peace and joy do not come naturally to fallen humankind, and we must daily make the choice to lean hard into them instead of the beckoning feelings of despair and sadness.

Dave encouraged me to take a look at Psalms, a place where David poured out laments to the Lord in his times of deepest despair. He told me to pay attention to the structure of the psalms to see the pattern of thought that David's laments revealed.

What we see in Psalms is David crying out to God, unafraid and unabashed in his raw emotions. Many times David questions God's purpose, presence, and plan. David does not hold back in pouring out the honest thoughts and feelings of his heart. But he does not leave them there.

David's psalms typically end on a note of praise, a willful acknowledgement that even though life is hard and God seems distant, He is worthy to be praised. He is worthy because He alone is our ultimate salvation and our ultimate source of peace. We can be confident in God's ability to be our comfort because even if death overtakes us, He has conquered the grave.

The book of Psalms was so deeply comforting to me during those difficult times because David reveals his humanness to the Father and God does not shrink from it. On the contrary, God allowed those raw laments to be included in His Holy Scriptures. The psalms helped me to see that David was in a desperate place many, many times and crying out for God's help with an honest admission of his true feelings. We can see this displayed in Psalm 6.

> Have mercy on me Lord, for I am faint, my bones are in agony … I am worn out from my groaning. All night long I flood my bed with weeping and drench

my couch with tears. My eyes grow weak with sorrow; they fail because of all my foes. [2]

Even David—a man after God's own heart, the anointed king of Israel—grew weak and weary in his agony. He poured out his laments to the Lord, knowing that Father God would hear him. We can confidently do the same. Speaker and author Vaneetha Rendall Risner writes this about lamenting to the Father,

> Lamenting keeps us engaged with God. When we lament, we invite God into our pain so that we can know His comfort, and others can see that our faith is real. Our faith is not a façade we erect to convince ourselves and others that pain doesn't hurt—it is an oak tree that can withstand the storms of doubt and pain in our lives, and grow stronger through them.[3]

God is not afraid of these raw emotions from a heart that is hurting deeply. It is okay to be weak and to come to the Father with all of our pain. In fact, He desires it. Just as an earthly father desires his child to come to him with the concerns of their heart, when we come to the Father in our pain, we are living out our dependence on Him. When we come to the Lord in weakness, we are made strong because of who He is and the power that He offers us.

During the months between Evie's diagnosis and her birth, my journal was filled time and time again with prayers of surrender over the things I could not control. There were so many unknowns about Evie's birth. Since we knew Evie's time with us would be short, I wanted everything to be perfect. I wanted to plan who would be there and when and how we would all get a chance to hold her. I wanted to plan exactly where Josh would be so he could be immediately available to hold his precious baby girl. I wanted to be surrounded by kind and compassionate doctors and staff at the time of my labor and delivery. I wanted Evie to be born alive. I tried to plan as best as I could, but really all I had was the realization that waiting was my only option. Wait and see. That was not the answer I wanted.

What I wanted instead—and still want today if I'm honest—was God's plan written out. A handwritten letter? An email maybe? Texts would definitely be acceptable. I could live life so much more comfortably if I only knew the plan. *I'll do anything, God! Just give me a little clue as to where this thing is going.*

But God does not want to do that for us. If He did, then we would be walking by sight and not by the faith that we so desperately need to cling to and that so blesses the heart of our Father.

Psalm 119:105 says, "Your word is a lamp to my feet and a light to my path." Do you know what I wish it said? "Your word is a crystal ball that shows my future so I can fully and appropriately plan for such." Or even "Your word is a flood lamp, illuminating the entire path and giving me an eagle-eye range of vision so I will never stumble or fall and the light will always eliminate the need to tread carefully." But the verse does not say that at all.

The picture that Psalm 119:105 paints in my mind is that of someone holding an ancient oil lamp, the kind that looks like Genie's lamp from Disney's *Aladdin*. The tiny opening at the end of the spout is where the fire would be, the only source of light. Imagine how carefully you would have to walk in order to navigate a pathway with only that small amount of light to guide you.

This is what God wants for us. He wants us to trust that the small amount of light He gives us is enough. He wants us to trust that He will give us sufficient light for our next couple of steps. He wants us to trust that He truly is the one guiding us. Ann Lamott says this about writing, but it certainly applies to life in general as well, "You don't have to see where you're going, you don't have to see your destination or everything you will pass along the way. You just have to see two or three feet ahead of you."[4] This is God's will for us.

One strategy that helped me tremendously in taming these anxious thoughts about the details of Evie's birth story was coming to the realization that God already had Evie's birth story planned out. Her birth story had already been written since the beginning of time and was providentially planned by our omnipotent Father.

Instead of focusing my attention on worry, I made every attempt to submit to the story God had written for my daughter and thank Him for what He already had planned. I began to thank God for the time we would have with her and the people who would be there. I began to thank Him for the story He wrote for her and us. I began to thank Him for what I knew was His best plan for our family, even though I was blind to the details of that plan and even if it were not what I would ultimately consider best. This was a very difficult exercise of faith and took an unbelievable amount of mental energy, but I was able to find comfort in choosing to rest in the Lord's sovereign plan.

Nancy Guthrie was faced with a similar crisis of faith when her daughter Hope was diagnosed with a rare and degenerative chromosomal disorder. In her book *Holding Onto Hope*, Nancy shares the comfort she found in submitting to God's will even if it were different than the story she would have chosen for her daughter.

> Because I believe God's plans for me are better than what I could plan for myself, rather than run away from the path He has set before me, I want to run toward it. I don't want to try and change God's mind—His thoughts are perfect. I want to think His thoughts. I don't want to change God's timing— His timing is perfect. I want the grace to accept His timing. I don't want to change God's plan—His plan is perfect. I want to embrace His plan and see how He is glorified through it. I want to submit.[5]

Another challenge during those months of my pregnancy was living with a constant sick feeling in the pit of my stomach over coming face-to-face with death. There was no picture I could paint in my mind that would make it easier to come home from the hospital with no baby. There was no online support group I could find that could tell me that watching my baby suffocate would not be agony. I lived in dread and trepidation of having a front-row seat to my child's death.

In those times the Lord would continually prompt my heart with a gentle thought: *But Sarah, what is true right now?* These words would ground me and tether me back down to reality, back to what was happening right in front of me.

What was true in those moments was that, right then and there, my baby girl was fine. She was moving and growing, and she was fine. Micah was happy, growing, and just as sweet as ever. And my husband was there, a sustaining presence in those tumultuous days. What was true right then, without projecting into the future at all, was that my life was fine. It took everything in me to anchor my thoughts down to those present moments and not be swept away by the raging current of dread.

It is true that God gives us grace to go through something, but He most certainly does not give us the grace to worry about it. Living a life of trust in the Lord means that we should think about today and live in light of eternity, but not expend precious mental energy worrying about the events of tomorrow. As Matthew 6:34 says, "Therefore, do not worry about tomorrow, for tomorrow will worry about its own things" (NKJV).

The disciplines of keeping my mind in the right place, trying to focus on thankfulness instead of anxiety over what was to come and continually hitting the reset button on my brain to focus on the present moment, were incredibly draining. A combination of these mind-wearying pursuits, the fact that I was pregnant and chasing around an almost two-year-old, and the reality that I shed a waterfall of tears every single day left me bone-tired. Each day was an emotional marathon.

One incredibly sweet gift the Lord gave me during that time was connection with other loss mothers through the blessing of online community. I began blogging regularly after Evie's diagnosis in order to keep loved ones updated with her prognosis and my pregnancy. But the blog also gave me the ability to connect with many other mothers who were going through similar situations. It was a comfort to know them and to know their stories. I felt a sense of solidarity in that community, knowing I was not alone in the heartbreak of my impending loss. These were friendships forged across states and sometimes oceans over sets of circumstances we never would have chosen for ourselves. Nonetheless, these women were a soft place for my heart to land.

In addition to those wonderful online friendships, I had a select few people in my real life who were crucial to my survival, women who would text me, call me, bring me coffee or dinner, and sit and cry with me. I fought all of the mental battles within my own head, but these wonderful people often handed me the weapons.

In her book *Looking for Lovely*, Annie F. Downs describes the importance of leaning on others in our most difficult life circumstances.

> I think of Exodus 17. Moses sends Joshua out to fight the Amalekites. As Joshua is out in the battle, if Moses's hands are raised, the Israelite army is winning. Any time he puts his hands down because his arms are tired, the Amalekites advance. So while Moses is standing at the top of the hill watching the battle below, they roll a rock over for him to sit on. And his brother Aaron and his brother-in-law Hur come and hold up his arms. They stayed beside him, holding up his arms, until the sunset. All. Day. Long.
>
> I love that visual. Having the people in your life that will hold you up when you are too tired to keep doing what you are called to do. It takes away some of the guilt I feel when I am tired to remember that Moses got tired too. Moses didn't try to do this on his own … he had to persevere—he had to keep his hands up even when he felt like he was unable to do it anymore—to ensure there was victory, but he couldn't do it alone. He needed his people.[6]

I am so deeply thankful to have been surrounded by such a committed band of those types of people, the kind who would always remember the hardship I was facing and do whatever they could do keep my arms raised high.

As the weeks pressed on following Evie's diagnosis, I tried to be intentional about making time for her. I would rub my belly and whisper sweet words to her, words about how she was loved so much and how I could not wait to kiss her face. Anytime I read to Micah or pushed him on the swing in our backyard, I tried to be intentional and acknowledge the fact that Evie was there and that she was doing it with us. I wanted to sear the memories of her presence with us in our daily lives onto my mind and my heart. It was all I would have this side of eternity.

One afternoon Josh and I were watching a movie. I was lounging on our sectional, the sweet spot where the two sides of the couch intersect into the most perfect, plushy corner. Josh was leaning lightly against me and my rounded belly. Suddenly, in what I assume was a wave of massive annoyance at the interference of her personal space, Evie kicked hard against Josh's back. She kicked so hard in fact that he jolted upright and looked at me, confused. The kick from our little belly baby girl was so hard and so direct that he thought I elbowed him in the ribs! We both laughed at our feisty little girl. It is my favorite memory of Evie, a little taste of what her personality might have been.

Life between July and November felt incredibly strange and surreal. It was the most bizarre mixture of normal and absolutely abnormal, of smiles and of overwhelming tears, of planning for our baby's arrival in a sacred, horrible, sweet, and dreadful way. Those days were not baby showers and crib assembly, but rather choosing the right burial site and funeral home. Instead of telling Evie my hopes and dreams about our life together, I whispered tearful, agonizing words to my girl, apologizing again and again for not having the ability to fix her.

Friends and family were kind and understanding. People reached out in all sorts of ways, the beautiful body of Christ, the hands and feet of Jesus working in a situation that needed tender care. God was faithful to reveal Himself to my heart as it fought for peace. He was also so faithful to demonstrate His provision through His people. We felt this provision in tangible ways, through meals and encouraging texts, and in intangible ways, like knowing our loved ones were interceding on our behalf to the throne of grace.

If I had to summarize what it was like in those four months, it would be a struggle to find those words. Because what word means pain plus peace plus agony plus knowing God's salvation is the ultimate and unrivaled comfort? But I think the truth of Isaiah 43:2 offers a pretty close encapsulation. "When you pass through the waters, I will be with you; And through the rivers, they shall not overflow you. When you walk through the fire, you shall not be burned, nor shall the flame scorch you" (NKJV).

Broken

We are too weak and too powerless to control even the most painful details of our own lives.

Beautiful

The Lord is truly near to the brokenhearted and does not shrink back from the evidences of our humanity that hard times reveal. He will meet us in our worry, our pain, and our questions. We will face hard times, but He will faithfully accompany us through the fire.

9

TRADES

> Approaching our difficulties from the standpoint of
> what I want, what I have lost, or what I think is fair
> will embitter us. Bitter eyes can perceive only the
> injustice and the sorrow in our situation. Grateful eyes,
> however, will always see the grace of God, regardless
> of how difficult our circumstances might be.[1]
>
> —Jennifer Rothschild

At about the twenty-seven-week mark of my pregnancy, I headed to the doctor's office for the standard gestational diabetes glucose test. The room I was sent to for the test was very small, with a single row of chairs pushed up against each side of the room and only enough space for a single-file walkway down the middle. I sat in a gray padded chair gripping a small plastic bottle containing the bright-red drink all pregnant women are destined to consume, the drink containing so much sugar that it almost seems carbonated. I cracked open the plastic safety lid and took my first sip. The liquid was syrupy sweet and slightly sickening.

"You have to drink the whole bottle within five minutes," the lab tech reminded me. Her words held all the enthusiasm of a person who had just been gifted a bag of cotton balls for her birthday.

After a few big gulps, I finally took one last miserable chug and let the lab tech know so she could start the clock on my one-hour wait time.

As I sat in that gray padded chair, I naturally looked around at my fellow waiting room inhabitants. There was a man to my right, quiet and possibly sleeping. There was a cute little family sitting across from me, a mama, daddy, and their eighteen-month-old daughter. They were expecting the arrival of a baby boy in the next few months. They were speaking Spanish, and the adorable little girl had big brown eyes just like Dora the Explorer and curly dark hair. I chatted with the mother about her pregnancy a bit, but when the conversation turned to me, I tried to keep my answers short. Friendly but short. It is really hard to talk to another pregnant woman about how your baby is going to die.

As I continued to scan the room, my eyes landed on the back right corner. I could see three people, two of them wearing khaki and brown and very official-looking law enforcement uniforms with wide-brimmed hats. I stared a little longer to get more details on the person sitting in between them. I could see a pair of rubber garden shoes and the very bottom hem of a pair of bright orange pants. And wrapped around the bottom of those bright orange pants was a pair of shiny metal ankle cuffs.

No, I thought. *I cannot be seeing what I think I am seeing!*

My eyes worked upward from the metal ankle cuffs to the rest of the orange jumpsuit and the wrists bound in handcuffs, and finally they landed on the face of a woman, worn and tired, her eyes emotionally vacant behind a pair of thin-rimmed glasses.

It took me a long time to make sense of what I saw. Like the dial-up internet of days gone by, my brain had to slowly and systematically link the incoming information together before making a worthwhile connection. The realization came, fuzzy at first, but soon locked into my mind with full clarity: this woman was a prison inmate. And she was pregnant.

Here in this waiting room, just a few chairs away from me, sat a pregnant female inmate. And, like me, she was probably awaiting the results of the same twenty-seven-week glucose test. My eyes continued to stare in her general direction long after the socially aware part of me knew I should stop. But I just sat there staring, trying desperately to process my speculations about her life situation juxtaposed against mine.

This woman was, by all contextual evidence, a criminal. She had made some, I'm guessing, less than stellar choices that landed her in jail. And she was also pregnant. The timeline of when she became pregnant in relation to her incarceration, I do not know. But she was unmistakably pregnant. And I made the generally safe assumption that her baby, like most of the babies growing inside their mamas in that waiting room, was healthy. Mine was not.

A sense of injustice burned like hot embers inside my chest. Here I sat, a nice girl who loved Jesus, carrying a baby girl that I desperately wanted to take home with me but would not be able to. And there, sitting just outside of my periphery, was a woman whose child would likely be taken from her and put into state custody after birth. Her baby would be another little person in need of love in an already overrun, overworked, and underfunded foster system.

Unbelievable.

My baby would die, and hers would live. If God had any sense of fairness, it just seemed right that we should switch. I assumed she wouldn't get to keep her baby anyway. Why did God also have to take mine? I didn't want her baby to die, per se. I just wanted my baby to live. And if God were going to take a baby, I would much rather it be hers.

Really, Lord? Really? Why couldn't we trade? Surely this woman doesn't need or want her baby like I want mine. She won't even be able to keep that baby! Why couldn't You just not give her a baby and give me mine instead? That feels so much more logical!

These thoughts were so wretchedly ugly, born out of a sense of entitlement from a person who forgot that what is actually fair for all of us is death, but only by the blood of Jesus do we have any chance at life. And forgetting that crucial piece about my wretchedness and the Lord's loveliness led me to envision the absurd untruth that somehow God had an infant death quota to meet and that taking the life of one baby was just as good as taking the life of another.

It would seem to my sin-tainted view of how the world should work and my rather self-serving perspective on justice that if God needed a story lived out where a baby was going to die, then He would take the baby from the mommy who would not get to keep her baby in the first place. But the Lord does not deal in these dark, black-market trades. The Lord is not just a bloodthirsty bounty hunter seeking the life of any baby. I cannot say, "Take hers and spare mine," and satisfy His plan. He does not work that way at all.

God knows His children intimately and desires for each one of us to be conformed more and more each day into the image of Jesus. He desires this for us so we can be the most effective for His kingdom, and so our obedience can receive the greatest blessing in eternity. And sometimes, this greatest good requires God to mold, form, and shape us in ways that are immensely uncomfortable and deeply painful.

In *Hinds' Feet In High Places*, the fragile Much-Afraid reflects on these words of the Good Shepherd.

> He had said, "Love is beautiful, but it is also terrible. Terrible in its determination to allow nothing blemished or unworthy to remain in the beloved."

> When she remembered this, Much-Afraid thought with a little shiver in her heart, "He will never be content until he makes me what he is determined that I ought to be."[2]

The Lord tailor-makes each person's story. It was part of my story to lose Evie and part of Evie's story to die so young. The intricate details of that suffering and the path I needed to take to endure it are part of the specific blueprint for my story, to smooth the rough edges unique to my personality in order to mold my heart closer and closer to the same shape of Christ's. It wouldn't do for the Lord to just take any baby. He needed to take my baby for the good of the gospel and for the good of His beloved daughter.

One reason that God allowed this type of hardship in my life is that He knew the particular discipline it would take for me to endure it would ultimately lead to a stronger, more beautiful character. As Hebrews 12:10–11 says, "For the moment all discipline seems painful rather than pleasant, but later it yields the peaceful fruit of righteousness to those who have been trained by it."

This is not discipline as in punishment, but discipline as it refers to vigilant monitoring, attention, and self-control to reach an ultimate goal. Just as a marathon runner must embrace a certain set of disciplines to ensure maximum performance at the big event, so the Lord often allows trials in our own lives to build our character, to ensure that our hearts can faithfully withstand the exertion of life in our fallen world.

And for the woman in the telltale orange jumpsuit? It is not a huge leap to assume that she had likely endured some hard things to get to the place where she was. Having that baby was part of her story. Maybe it was part of her redemption story. Sometimes I think of her and pray for her and hope very much that her life has been changed for the better and that maybe she has come to know the God who gave each one of us sweet little babies.

A few years before she passed away, my dear friend Darla's grandmother, Clarene Shantz, gifted each member of her family with a keepsake self-made autobiography. It contained beautiful stories, memories, and details of their precious family. But it was also saturated with the deep, rich faith that poured so gracefully from Grandma Shantz's life as she walked out the story God had written for her, the faith she hoped to pass along to future generations.

In one section of the family memoir, Grandma Shantz talks about the difficulty of losing her eighteen-year-old son, Greg, to a terrible industrial accident. She titled this section of her memoir *Lessons Learned from Grief* and reflected on how she too struggled with feeling as though God was not acting fairly when He took her son.

> "I inquired of God, 'Why my son?' His answer in the form of a question was clear.

'Would you rather I had taken another mother's son, who perhaps didn't know Me?'

Immediately I repented for the selfishness and pride that prompted my questions. The implication of that sort of questioning is, 'I'm too good and I don't deserve that sort of treatment and heartache.' The truth is that I, a sinner, deserve hell."[3]

When the question of our hearts becomes "Why not them?" it reveals an ugliness deep within, an ugliness born from a sense of entitlement and blindness to our own need for Jesus. The woman with the orange jumpsuit and me with my dying belly baby, we both deserve nothing more than hell. But God loved us both so much that He made a way through Jesus. How could I be so rotten as to feel entitled to more?

As author and speaker Jennifer Rothschild writes, "In our pre-Christ state, we only deserved hell because sin deserves hell. Sin is not worthy of heaven. If not for Christ, we would have received the full weight of what our sin deserved. But, Christ took what He did not deserve so we would never have to."[4]

God is not interested in trades. He is not interested in just anyone dying or living, struggling or thriving, or seeking or finding. He wants certain people to walk certain paths, just like He needed me to carry my heaven-bound Evie-girl. And for reasons unknown to me, He needed that orange-clad woman to carry and birth her own baby. Honestly though, no matter which way you slice that pie, I don't think any person with eyeballs and half a heart would have labeled the slice of pie on my plate as "fair."

But I, for one, am so very thankful that God does not go for fair. What He goes for is love. A love so deep it carved a way out of eternal death and destruction. A love so grand that it penned a personal story for each one of us, filled with thousands of opportunities to demonstrate our love and faithfulness in return. 2 Corinthians 4:16–18 offers such encouragement for suffering hearts in light of what it means for our eternal reality.

> So we do not lose heart. Though our outer self is wasting away, our inner self is being renewed day by day. For this light momentary affliction is preparing for us an eternal weight of glory beyond all comparison, as we look not to the things that are seen but to the things that are unseen. For the things that are seen are transient, but the things that are unseen are eternal.

Few things grieved me like the impending loss of my sweet baby girl. But I have full confidence that nothing will give me greater joy than to stand before my God knowing that, instead of trading my life for a more comfortable one, He pushed me forward and allowed me the opportunity to live the life that would allow for the greatest fellowship with Him for all of eternity.

God never promised comforts in this life or dreams come true. He never promised fair. What He has promised, however, is a reward for those who stay faithful, even when they're asked to walk a path they would never have chosen, a path they would have given anything to trade if given the chance. And because of Jesus, He promises life, ten thousand times over, to a world full of undeserving souls.

Broken

This world does not operate in a way that we, as fallen humans, would label as fair or just.

Beautiful

We are deeply thankful that God does not operate in fair because we are freely given something we do not deserve, and we are given countless opportunities to allow ourselves to be molded into the type of person whose character is most pleasing in His eyes and most worthy of reward in our eternal existence.

10

BE GLORIFIED IN THIS PLACE

'Tis so sweet to trust in Jesus,
Just to take Him at His Word;
Just to rest upon His promise,
And to know, "Thus saith the Lord!¹"

—Louisa M. R. Stead,
'Tis So Sweet to Trust in Jesus

As the days on the calendar creeped closer and closer to Evie's due date, I found myself in such an intense mind battle with the enemy who wanted nothing more than to tear me down, bit by weary bit, until all that was left was a mere robotic shell. One of the only ways I found to combat his attacks was to stream praise and worship music through my house all day.

One afternoon I was drowning in an especially emotionally weary moment where I repeatedly begged God to allow this cup—this difficulty—to pass from me. The time for Evie's birth was near, and I dreaded the heartbreaking events that were to come. I prayed and wept to the Lord, pouring my brokenness before His throne. In the midst of my prayer, my ears tuned into a familiar song—one of my very favorites—as it played from my laptop. It was a song called "Knees to the Earth" by the husband-and-wife duo known as Watermark.

The powerful words of the song washed over me. The Holy Spirit moved through me as only He can and focused my attention on the tender strength of the song lyrics. The Spirit used the song to push my heart to let go of everything I feared. He moved me to surrender, to choose to glorify the Lord in the place I was in. I dropped to my knees and lifted my hands high in the air, face wet with tears of bittersweet surrender as the holy words played around me.

> Beautiful Jesus, how may I bless Your heart?
> Knees to the earth I bow down to everything
> You are Beautiful Jesus, You are my only worth
> So let me embrace You always as I walk this earth
> Be blessed, be loved, be lifted high
> Be treasured here, be glorified
> I owe my life to You my Lord
> Here I am[1]

I sang and beg-prayed the line "Be treasured *here*, be glorified!" over and over as the song continued to play.

The "here" part was the part where I felt the most pain, the part from within where I knew God was calling me to worship. My "here" was living in a place—in a space in time—where I was pregnant with a precious baby girl who was going to die. I needed to treasure the Lord and everything He had done for me and would do for me right here in this place where my heart was splayed open and seeping lifeblood.

I would have given absolutely anything in those days to hear a word of healing from the doctors. I would have given so much of my own comfort just to hear the words, "Remarkably, unbelievably, healed!" spoken by the sonographers at the next ultrasound appointment. But what I was faced with instead of healing was the choice—an opportunity really—to fall on my face before a holy God who can be praised despite our circumstances. But this is far from easy.

It feels so much better to find the words and melodies of praise when my heart feels like sunshine: optimistic, warm, and promising. I feel like praising when I feel good and happy. But when outside the window all I see is a thick layer of storm clouds, my heart tends toward darkness and questioning God's purposes.

Something incredibly sacred happens, however, in the soul that chooses to praise despite the darkness and the raging deluge of questions. There is a sweetness to that surrender, echoing the sweetest surrender of our own Jesus in the garden of Gethsemane just before He was arrested the night before His crucifixion. "And He knelt down and prayed saying, 'Father, if it is Your will, take this cup away from Me; nevertheless not My will, but Yours be done'" (Luke 22:41–42).

And lest we think that it was easy for Jesus—the God-Man—to surrender and beat ourselves up over how difficult it is to choose surrender when our hearts are aching, the story in the garden continues. "And being in agony, He prayed more earnestly. Then His sweat became like great drops of blood falling down to the ground" (Luke 22:44).

God the Son was in agony as His heart prepared for the dreadful events of His death on the cross. Jesus's heart desperately wanted to surrender and glorify the Lord, which was right. But that did not make surrender any easier. As my friend Holly says, "I think God is glorified in our fight to surrender, even if it is an ugly fight."[2]

This act of surrender, of willfully attempting to choose alignment with the Lord's plans for our lives even when they hurt is an act of true worship to our heavenly Father. Vaneetha Rendell Risner's testimony holds real evidence to such.

Before the age of thirteen, Vaneetha had undergone twenty-one surgeries in attempts to make her life with polio just a little more livable. As a young wife and mother, she lost several babies to miscarriage and also walked the painful road of infant loss when her son Paul died at two months old from an oversight from a pediatric cardiologist.

A few years later, Vaneetha developed severe pain from post-polio syndrome, and her health began to deteriorate rapidly. Her husband decided it was all too much to deal with and left Vaneetha to raise her two teenage daughters alone. It is fair to say this woman has endured the stuff of most of our nightmares, the sort of trials that leave all of us weepy and wondering why God does this to hearts committed to Him.

Vaneetha's life has been immensely hard and marked by deep suffering and pain. But while this woman has some incredible experiences to list on her suffering résumé and enough baggage to call it quits with regards to finding joy in the midst of hard times, she is a strong voice in the power of God's sustaining grace during trials and His supernatural promise of inexplicable joy in the midst of Mariana Trench-level pain.

In her book *The Scars That Have Shaped Me*, Vaneetha talks about the sacred dance of surrender as worship.

> I think about [the] moment by moment surrenderings. [The] choice to be grateful when things are not perfect. [The] dying to self. These are acts of worship. They have eternal significance. I realize that all my responses matter as well. I can show the surpassing worth of Christ when I suffer well, when I joyfully accept circumstances that are less than perfect, when I lay down my need to control. Giving up my right to have something exactly as I want can be an act of worship.[4]

Just like Vaneetha, as my life became more and more acquainted with grief, I realized just how much of a conscious choice it was to surrender to the will of God. When life felt easy, it felt easy to surrender to God's good will because His good will would yield good things. But when faced with the impending death of my baby girl, it became so much harder to see how surrender would yield good and easier to want to turn my heart in the opposite direction.

One night shortly after Evie's diagnosis, I was kneeling beside our bathtub, adjusting the faucet so the water would be just the right temperature for Micah's bath. As I swirled the water in a figure-eight motion with my hand, I became fixated on this idea that there was no way in the world God would let my baby girl die. I mentally stomped my foot down—*hard*—and let God know exactly what I thought of His wretched little plan.

There is no way, God! There is no way You are going to make me do this. I can't. I just can't, and You can't let it happen! And that is final. No further discussion necessary!

Immediately I began to break down and cry. I sobbed so hard that it became difficult to catch my breath. A reality crashed over me that I simply did not want to face.

In my mind, I saw a distinct crossroads. Both roads led to the same result, the death of my baby girl. There was nothing I could do and nothing the medical professionals could do that would save her life. It was up to me which road I would take to arrive at that same dismal end.

Would I choose the road that would glorify the Lord? Would I choose the path of willful—albeit agonizing—surrender, a path that would give weight to everything I ever said I believed about God and His Word? Or would I choose the other path, the one where I rebelled against God in any way I could, turning angry and bitter at this story He wrote for my life and for the life of my little girl?

I had a very distinct choice. Would I surrender to the good will of a good Father, even though it all felt so bad? Or would I go my own way and follow the darkness no matter how far it took me? The choice was mine to make.

While it was always evident from the onset of her diagnosis that Evie's physical condition would not be healed (barring a complete and utter miracle), it was a realization that took me some time to come to grips with. I wrote this in my journal just a few short weeks after her diagnosis:

> *Painful realization this morning—one I think I always knew but didn't want to face head on: Evie isn't meant to be healed.*

> *Since we heard the news, I have been so vocal about the journey. So many people are being reached for Christ. As [a mentor] said, I have a platform now, and people are*

listening. Women are emailing me and finding comfort in my words. Even [family member's name] has been challenged to rethink their faith abandonment. I really feel the Lord is using me and wants to see this to the end. (Phil 1:6)

I have prayed—begged really—for healing for my baby. Those prayers somehow seem hollow compared to the ones for peace and wisdom and direction. I really think God is preparing my heart for goodbye.

I desperately don't want it, but I think it is inevitable. When I pray for strength to say goodbye, I can almost hear an audible voice say "I will help you," not "You won't have to." I'm so, so afraid, but I am trusting.

I had been asking for God to use me and give me a place to really shine for Him. He gave one to me. I just didn't realize how much it would cost. But I have sung "Take It All" and "Take My Life and Let It Be." Did I really mean it? If so … so be it, all for God's glory.

Channels only, blessed Master, but with all they wondrous pow'r, flowing through us, Thou canst use us, every day, and every hour.*

There is something sacred about surrendering our will to the Father even when it hurts. The Lord can be glorified in the place where surrender meets a heart actively breaking, and faith is most decidedly itself when we move forward—tears streaming and soul crushing under the weight of reality—and make the choice anyway to praise the God of our salvation. When we choose to surrender to the will of God no matter how difficult things are, we build a strong and powerful testimony right before the eyes of a world begging to see.

Paul says that when we suffer in this life, we enter into fellowship with the suffering of Christ. We can understand Christ and His sacrifice of love on a different level when we enter into those hard things with eternal eyes, even if we must strain our eyes to see just a faint outline of what that deeper fellowship might be. As Paul writes, "For it has been granted to you that for the sake of Christ you should not only believe in him but also suffer for his sake."[5]

Helen Roseveare is often referred to as a woman of whom the world was not worthy. Helen was a doctor with a heart for medical missions. She poured her life into serving the people of the Congo, Africa, and was especially known for her work with mothers, children, and those affected with leprosy.

In 1964, the Congo broke out in civil war, and hostile rebel forces imprisoned Helen and ten other missionaries. These captors were most vile and heartlessly cruel, beating Helen and her fellow captives with fists, steel-toed boots, the butt ends of rifles, and rubber truncheons. On October 29, 1964, Helen Roseveare was brutally raped.

Even though Helen had offered up her life in full service to the Lord as a medical missionary, she struggled to make sense of these horrific experiences. She questioned the Lord and His purposes. She wondered why He had not stepped in to stop these appalling events. As the Lord often does, He met Helen in her pain. Helen relays what she sensed as the Lord's response to her heart in those wretched moments. "You asked Me, when you were first converted, for the privilege of being a missionary. This is it. Don't you want it? These are not your sufferings. They're Mine. All I ask of you is the loan of your body."[6]

With a faith that towers over anything I could claim, Helen later reflects on the message she heard from the Lord after that brutal attack.

> One word became unbelievably clear, and that word was privilege. He didn't take away pain or cruelty or humiliation. No! It was all there, but now it was altogether different. It was with Him, for Him, in Him. He was actually offering me the inestimable privilege of sharing in some little way the edge of the fellowship of His suffering.

In the weeks of imprisonment that followed and in the subsequent years of continued service, looking back, one has tried to "count the cost," but I find it all swallowed up in privilege. The cost suddenly seems very small and transient in the greatness and permanence of the privilege.[5]

When we consider the great ways in which the Lord Jesus suffered for our sake, it seems only fitting that we would willingly enter into suffering as He did, for the benefit of His kingdom. Following the example of Christ, we should allow our attitude to be one of sweet surrender and worship. When we choose to surrender—to suffer well when every fiber within us screams for another way—we enter into the same suffering as our precious Savior, the One who sweat drops of blood in agony over the way His body would break for our salvation.

Broken

The world is full of suffering and painful experiences that can rob us of joy and motivation to surrender our own will to the Lord.

Beautiful

When we choose to surrender, even when we do not want to, the Lord is glorified, and we experience a sweetness in the surrender and the sacred privilege of suffering for His sake.

FEARFULLY AND
WONDERFULLY MADE

See from His head, His hands, His feet,
Sorrow and love flow mingled down!
Did e'er such love and sorrow meet,
Or thorns compose so rich a crown?[1]

—Isaac Watts, *When I Survey The Wondrous Cross*

Thursday, November 8, 2012, started in the most dreadful way. I woke up around four in the morning from a terrible nightmare where I dreamed that my one-year-old son had fallen down into an open manhole. I was screaming for help, but no one could hear me. In the dream, I was vividly faced with this dilemma: jump in with him and run the risk that no one would find us or leave my desperate, frightened son alone in the hole to go find help. I woke up with my heart pounding and tears in my eyes. The angst of my troubled pregnancy reached even into my dreams.

I fell back asleep for a couple more hours on the couch in the living room, pillows surrounding and supporting every swollen inch of my thirty-seven-week pregnant body. Besides the discomfort of a full-term pregnancy, I had trouble finding a restful position because I had been experiencing some very intense Braxton-Hicks contractions for the last ten days.

Doctors, pregnancy books, and even Google will tell you that Braxton-Hicks contractions should not be painful. They are really only practice contractions that allow a pregnant woman's body to gear up for the real-deal contractions, the ones that will help birth the baby. However, what the books, doctors, and even Google will not tell you is that if you have no amniotic fluid due to a fatal genetic anomaly in your sweet baby and therefore no fluid to cushion these so-called "practice" contractions, they will be uncomfortable. They will be very, very uncomfortable.

That was how my morning began: shaking off a nightmare, suffering in pain from these irregular contractions, caring for my baby boy, and dealing with the emotions of the anticipated arrival and subsequent death of my baby girl.

After a quick breakfast, Micah and I went to the grocery store. We came home, had lunch, napped, and then spent the rest of the day playing outside in the beautiful fall weather. I even had enough energy to rake up several piles of crunchy fall leaves. But by the time I went to make dinner that night, my contractions felt quite a bit stronger than they had earlier in the day. I made an attempt to time them and determine if I were perhaps in active labor, but could not detect a regular, timeable pattern. I tried to write the contractions off as mere Braxton-Hicks, but something inside of me feared they were something more.

A bit later at the dinner table, I tried to choke down some forkfuls of pasta, but the anxious feeling in the pit of my stomach made it hard to swallow.

Josh stared at me. "What's wrong?" he asked in a very concerned tone.

"I don't know. I might be in labor" was my weak and tentative reply.

Josh suggested I lie down and try to time the contractions again. But once again, there was no predictable timing pattern. In my mind, this meant I was not yet in active labor. Also in my mind was the fact that I still had three weeks left until my due date. My OB doctors had alluded to the fact that because my baby was small and because the lack of amniotic fluid made my stomach smaller than the average pregnancy belly, I ran a greater chance of being overdue than going into early labor. All of these details led me to conclude that birthing a baby that night was not a real possibility.

I bathed Micah, rocked him, and put him to bed. I attempted dinner a second time but just could not bring myself to eat. With the contractions still coming, I wondered if I were on the precipice of active labor. I decided that taking a bath might help. The midwives always recommend taking a bath to help determine whether or not a mom is in active labor. The warm water will either stop contractions or speed them up, depending on whether or not a mother is truly in labor. In the forty-five minutes I was in the bathtub, I had only two contractions. Once again, I wrote the contractions off as false labor and began to get ready for bed. I was not completely certain that was the right choice.

Josh walked into our bedroom just in time to see me leaning over our bed breathing heavily through another contraction.

"Um, those are not Braxton-Hicks," he said knowingly, having experienced labor with me before.

"I know," I said, "but they still aren't regular!" I was confused and in pain and borderline in tears.

Josh encouraged me to lie down and relax and try, once more, to time the contractions.

Between 10:00 p.m. and 10:30 p.m., I had four very regular contractions. The intensity was much stronger and required a greater level of focus and concentration to endure. I recalled feeling this very same way during my active labor stage with Micah. After wiping the sweat from my upper lip, I determined that this was finally and definitively real labor.

I got up out of bed to tell Josh to call his family so they could come over and watch Micah so we could leave for the hospital. He nodded and dialed his mom's cell phone. I decided to try to go to the bathroom one last time before we left.

As soon as I sat down on the toilet, I felt the undeniable urge to push.

"Ohhhh no!" I moaned. I could not believe what was happening.

I hoisted myself to a standing position and walked as quickly as I could toward the bathroom door yelling, "Josh, we have to leave for the hospital now! The baby is coming!"

Josh looked at me, eyes wide, and then yelled into the phone for his parents to nix the original plan and just meet us at the hospital. I shuffled my way into our room to gather our bags.

In the midst of the flurry of throwing things into bags and changing clothes, I tried to call the doctor and tell him we were on our way. Instead I had to thrust the phone into Josh's hands as the overwhelming feeling of a very productive contraction took control of my entire body, every muscle fiber laser-focused on the fire tearing through my lower abdomen. I dropped to my knees, and the sound of my primal moans filled our room.

I managed to make it the few steps from our bedroom into the living room and collapsed again on my knees, this time in front of the couch. I buried my face into the cool leather as another contraction took possession of my body and I moaned again, the absolutely involuntary kind that accompanies the transition stage of labor right before full dilation and subsequent pushing. But my body must have been working in overdrive because suddenly the urge to push was so overwhelming and so incredibly strong, as if my body were shoving my will aside and moving forward with the birthing process whether I participated or not.

In a moment of disbelief, I reached down under my nightgown and felt the unmistakable warmth of a baby's skull on my fingertips.

"Josh! Call the ambulance!" I screamed. "She is coming right now! I can feel her, Josh! She is coming *right now!*"

Josh yelled back at me from the bedroom, "No! We are not having this baby here! Get in the car!"

Looking back this memory makes me chuckle, because I am convinced that only my enneagram eight husband would demand that his wife control her own labor, resist her body's undeniable urge to push a baby out, and get in the car for a twenty-minute car drive to the hospital. But he was right to do it.

Because of Evie's condition, we had no idea what to expect with labor or what sort of care she would need immediately after birth. We needed to be somewhere with people, tools, equipment, and knowledge. We needed the hospital.

Somehow I was able to maneuver my laboring body down our front steps and out to the car, but not before screaming out in pain and anguish over the absolute lack of control I had over every single aspect of my life in that moment.

I flung open the car door and stared at the passenger's seat. There was absolutely no way I could assume a sitting position. My pelvis was filled with a baby, and my hips truly could not bend that way at that particular moment in time. So I held onto the door frame of the car, heaved my giant body onto the seat backward, and knelt, arms around the headrest, pressing my face into the cushion. Josh took his place behind the wheel after securing little Micah into his car seat.

"We're taking Mommy to the hospital!" Josh told Micah excitedly, as if his voice alone could undo the frantic pace of the situation.

"Drive fast," I whispered to Josh as he sped away from our little home.

Josh spoke a prayer over all of us as he pressed his foot down, pedal to the metal, and headed toward the hospital. Praise God there were no law enforcement officers along the way and plenty of green lights because I am not so sure we would have made it otherwise. I don't recall very much from that car ride, save for some excited comments from Micah in the back seat about Daddy driving a racecar and the distinct awareness that a few sets of contractions notably did not happen as they should have, given the stage of labor I was in during that drive. Thank you, Jesus.

Josh pulled up to the hospital's ER entrance and rushed in to get help. I made it to the hospital without having a baby in the car, but just barely. As soon as my feet hit the concrete walkway leading up to the double doors, I could no longer resist the urge to push. The first half of Evie's head emerged. I hobbled toward the security guard, who was standing behind a wheelchair meant for me.

I tried to contort my laboring body containing a partially birthed baby as best I could into the wheelchair and pleaded to the security guard, "Please go quickly! This baby is coming, and she needs help!"

Now I know what I said to him was meant to have the effect of "Ride like the wind!" but he must have heard something very different because this kind sir meandered my wheelchair down the hallway with all the speed of a geriatric turtle. Nothing could have prepared either one of us for what happened next.

In what felt like one swift motion, accompanied by a guttural scream, I pushed Evie's body out. I reached down into my leggings and pulled her up onto my lap. My first look at my precious girl and her purple-blue coloring told me that she was not well.

The security guard (whom we have since christened Leroy because we cannot seem to remember this poor guy's name and whom I am absolutely certain we scarred for life) uttered a quiet, "Whoa."

Leroy picked up his speed a little, but thankfully the ER charge nurse intercepted us in the hallway. She locked onto the urgency of my situation, grabbed hold of the wheelchair, and began sprinting toward her medical team. She was calling, "Blue baby! Blue baby!" over her radio system.

By the time we made it down to the ER room, the room was buzzing with an entire team of people waiting to care for my baby and me. However, not one of these wonderful people knew anything about me, my pregnancy, or the fatal diagnosis of my sweet girl.

I paused for half a second to take everything in and wondered how on earth we got there. Josh and I had been so careful to meet with a neonatologist—a kind man with great skill in situations like ours—who would make himself and his NICU team available when I went into labor. There was a children's hospital attached to the hospital where I would deliver so, should any special life-saving measures need to be taken, we were in close proximity to the best that modern medicine had to offer. And we had been so careful to discuss the fact that we just wanted palliative care for our baby girl, no wires or tubes, just her as she was. We knew our time would be short and wanted to treasure her—just her—as long as we could. But now we were thrust into this situation where not a single person in the room knew what we had spent months preparing for and poring over with the most skilled professionals. It was all indescribably overwhelming.

The doctors and nurses tried to get some information from me. They were asking what I wanted done for my baby who was an unhealthy blue color and obviously not processing oxygen as she should be. I tried, quite unsuccessfully, to make words come out of my mouth. Then I heard Josh's voice from behind me. He instantly began barking out our DNR (Do Not Resuscitate) orders and our desire for palliative care measures only.

The only problem was that the medical team had no idea who this man was! And since it was pretty obvious I was this baby's mother (if having an umbilical cord stretching from inside your body to the belly button of another human being doesn't prove your maternity, I don't know what does), I was the only one they wanted to hear from. Even still, I was so overwhelmed that I struggled to form words into cohesive sentences.

Finally I blurted out, "I don't know! Talk to my husband. He knows everything!"

With that, the staff motioned Josh into the room, and at his direction, they snipped the umbilical cord. I was taken to one side of the room and Evie to another.

The nurses asked me a lot of questions about my prenatal care and my OB doctor. After my answers were verified in their system and they understood the severity of our situation, their treatment and tone went from all business to kind and compassionate. I remember holding my hands up, dirty from blood and birth, and asking one of the nurses if she could please clean them off so I could hold my baby. She smiled kindly, brought over some warm rags, and wiped my hands clean.

As soon as I was given the all-clear and changed from my soiled street clothes into a hospital gown, the nurses wheeled my bed over to where Evie was being cared for. Josh was standing over her, watching as only a daddy can, as the pediatric doctor hand-pumped oxygen into her body through a tiny mask on her face. When Josh saw me, he walked over to me and gave me a quiet smile.

"Is she ok?" I asked hesitantly.

"Yes, she is fine," he assured me. "As soon as they started giving her oxygen, she pinked up. She looks good for now." His eyes were peaceful as he gave the report.

I will never forget the moment the doctor handed that sweet little girl to me. She was wrapped in the standard white newborn hospital blanket, the one striped with blue and pink. The tiniest oxygen mask was strapped onto her mouth and nose. As soon as she was in my arms, I kissed her adorable, chubby face. Evie's cheeks were so soft and so plump. I kissed her as gently as I could, trying not to move that oxygen mask because if there were any chance it was extending her life, you had better believe I was not moving it even one half of one inch. I could not stop kissing this sweet girl, this girl for whom we had prayed for months and months. She was finally here.

I lay flat on the hospital bed, which made it hard to see Evie's whole face. But once we were transferred to an ER recovery room, my bed was elevated to a more comfortable position, and I was finally able to look on my girl in her entirety.

Up until this point, I had been afraid of what Evie might look like. I knew that babies with oligohydramnios (lack of amniotic fluid) exhibit a set of physical symptoms known as Potter's Sequence. This sequence can include irregularities in the nose, ears, skin, and feet. And I had been able to tell from the many ultrasounds we had previously that her head was abnormally cone-shaped, likely due to her head-down position and the lack of fluid suspension. I didn't know what she would look like, and I worried that I would be incredibly shocked by her appearance. But she was immediately beautiful to me.

One look at this precious baby girl would have certainly revealed that something was very wrong with her. Her skin was not a healthy pink, but a blueish-purple tone, a result of her hypoplastic lungs and her oddly developed heart and their inability to work together to properly oxygenate her body. Her wrists and hands were bent severely inward, likely the result of months of development inside her cramped conditions. She was broken. That much was plainly obvious. But no level of brokenness could steal this mama's magnetic affections.

Evie had such plump cheeks, and I could not stop caressing her face and nuzzling my own face against her newborn softness. She also had such perfectly shaped lips. They were her daddy's lips, the very ones I am still so fond of kissing. Her nose looked a lot like Micah's did when he was born, a little wider set and perfect for—you guessed it—kissing. She was beautiful. She was broken and yet so incredibly beautiful. And she was mine. I loved her instantly.

Shortly after my transfer to the ER recovery room, our family and the handful of friends we had invited to come and meet Evie filed into the room. Even Josh's youngest brother, who had just randomly decided to come home from college for the weekend, was able to arrive at the hospital at exactly the same time as everyone else.

It was so sweet to watch our loved ones hold our girl. We were all weepy for what we knew was to come, but equally joyful for this precious gift. I wanted to be brave for Evie; she made me want to be brave. I tried to do my very best to convey a lifetime of love and affection in just a few short minutes. My friend Chani was there, diligently and skillfully snapping photos of us the entire time.

After Evie made the rounds to her adoring fans, Josh and I were able to give her a little sponge bath and dress her in the white layette outfit I had picked out, the one with a trio of flowers embroidered on the collar. I felt such a deep sense of pride when I was able to crown her with a soft pink headband, one I had crafted carefully with my own hands.

One of my favorite memories of that night was the moment Micah gave his new little sister the plush ladybug toy I previously picked out for him to gift her when she arrived. As much as I could beforehand, I prepped his little twenty-two-month-old mind for what to expect. I told him many times that when baby Evie came, he could give her this special toy and give her a hug and a kiss. He was so excited to do this for his little sister … until the moment came and he felt all eyes on him. And then, instead of handing the plush toy to her gently and planting a tender kiss on her forehead, as I had so dreamily envisioned, he just tossed the toy in her general direction and went about his own business. That memory still makes me chuckle.

We all laughed and smiled where we could, trying hard to beat back the reality of why we were all there. In one moment that was as equally heart-wrenching as it was sacred, Josh's dad led the room in a round of the "Happy Birthday" song. We tried to smile through it, but a somberness fell over the room as we realized this would be the one and only time we would ever sing "Happy Birthday" to Evie on this earth.

After a couple of hours, our group was transferred to a recovery room on the mother-baby unit. It was a significantly smaller room, but our supportive band of friends and family followed us nonetheless. We took a few more pictures, including one with me holding both of my babies, two precious hearts beating right next to mine. It had been a dream of mine, and so many people prayed that it would be possible. Praise God for that gift.

Not long after we entered into that second recovery room, Evie began to show signs of serious decline. We noticed her breathing had become very labored, with longer spans between each inhale and exhale and a haunting, rattling sound following each one.

I held Evie as close to me as I could. Josh wrapped his arms around both of us. He and I sat there in the hospital bed, hanging onto one other, desperately clinging to each another for strength to face the inevitability that this sweet little life would leave us very, very soon.

No human language possesses adequate words to describe what it feels like to watch as life slowly leaves your newborn baby. I have never felt so palpably and sickeningly helpless in my entire life. I was strong like wet tissue paper is strong. The moment felt like a horrible dream, the kind where you're trying to yell and warn someone of something incredibly important, but no sound can escape your lips. Instead you are left mute, but still trying desperately to speak. Except this bad dream was my reality.

I felt myself hanging onto Evie's every breath as the time between inhales and exhales increased. I hoped so desperately she was not in any pain, that she wasn't uncomfortable. But I can't imagine a scenario where suffocating to death is at all comfortable.

As I watched the life inside of my baby girl fade, I sang softly to her, right into her tiny ear so no one else could hear.

> Some glad morning when this life is over
> I'll fly away
> To that home on God's celestial shore
> I'll fly away
> I'll fly away, oh glory
> I'll fly away in the morning
> When I die, Hallelujah by and by
> I'll fly away[2]

I've heard that sometimes people who are dying hang on to their last bit of life just for the sake of their loved ones, as if they need permission from that loved one that it is ok to slip into the eternal. I was not sure if Evie needed that, but just in case, I leaned in even closer and whispered with a shaky voice, "Fly to Jesus, sweet girl. It's ok."

I watched as Evie inhaled and then exhaled, slow and labored. And then one lonely exhale.

I waited a few moments before touching her sweet little lips. She tended to move her lips if I touched them. It was a sign that she was still with us. But her lips remained still. I continued to rub my fingers gently over her lips, hopeful for even the tiniest movement.

"I think Evie is gone," Josh whispered.

I nodded and squeezed my eyes shut tight. And then Josh and I broke down in fits of whole-body sobs. We wept so hard that the hospital bed shook with our grief. Death had just stolen our newborn baby. My heart felt ripped open and torn apart. Nothing had ever felt crueler. For the first time in my life, I had a keen awareness that death and evil are actual, real, and the most loathsome of enemies. My entire being felt sick.

But despite this deep, deep pain, perhaps what strikes me most about the night Evie came and died was that our time with her was not entirely sad. It was sorrow and love flowing, mingled down, just as it did the night Christ died for all of us, just like the night death overtook the Savior of the world while He simultaneously worked to overturn its power.

That night we sat on the edge of something sacred, the truest wrinkle in time where two worlds meet, the one where death is an enemy that steals the dearest people from us, and the one where their souls spend forever in a glorious eternity. It was surreal and palpable all at once. It was horrible and yet somehow holy.

My dear friend Lauren was there the night Evie came. She had been such a good friend to me in those months between Evie's diagnosis and arrival, always willing to talk, to listen, to share, and to cry with me. The next day after coming home from the hospital, Lauren gave me the best gift a mother who just lost her baby girl could ask for: the most thoughtful, meaningful retelling of what my Evie meant to her and what that night had looked like from her perspective. It was Lauren's own personal retelling of the holy intertwining of both grief and joy that we all felt that blessed night.

> *Evie Caris may have arrived in a hurry, but the time that followed was nothing less than holy. To be able to celebrate, rejoice, and soak up every moment of her life with those who loved her was such a gift. From her sweet little meow noises, her little fingers and toes, her lips blowing bubbles, to her warm ball of softness … we got to experience the miracle of life.*

> *I will never forget the way Evie felt in my arms or the sweet hiccups she got as I held her. I got to snuggle her and gaze at her through blurry eyes.*

> *In the most perfect of moments, you allowed us to watch a heavenly thing. In that little room, it seemed as though all of heaven waited with bated breath for their newest member. As Josh wrapped his arms around you and Evie, you sang your sweet girl right into the presence of Jesus. Sacred. Holy. Beautiful. I will never forget the peace and*

*beauty that encompassed her after she left for heaven …
or the feel of her soft cheeks as I kissed her goodbye.*

*I looked out my window this morning to see the world
rushing by. Didn't they know a miracle had happened?
Didn't they know that the sacred touched down in the
wee hours of the morning? Time has stopped for a little
while. I know it must start again, but I don't want to
miss God in this moment. I want to cherish everything
this experience is. I will never forget.*

*Evie Caris came and touched hearts and lives. In just
four hours, her life made an impact that some never do. I
will always remember the way she felt in my arms … the
way she looked in yours … and I will always remember
her home going and the love in that room.*

*Tonight as I wrap my daughter in her pink blanket, I
will pray for your broken mommy heart, and I will praise
and worship the Father for precious Evie Caris … your
daughter … a gift from the Lord.*

Broken

Death is a true enemy that causes the deepest grief and robs us of time
with much-loved friends and family members.

Beautiful

There is a sacred place where joy and sorrow meet because for those of
us in Christ, this life is not the end. The sacred, holy place of a soul on
the precipice of eternity ushers those of us on earth into a deep sense
of worship and adoration for the Father who, through Jesus, made
provision for eternal life.

12

THE COMFORT AND
HOPE OF HEAVEN

Meanwhile, we on this dying Earth can relax and rejoice for our loved ones who are in the presence of Christ. Our parting is not the end of our relationship, only an interruption. We have not "lost" them, because we know where they are. They are experiencing the joy of Christ's presence in a place so wonderful that Christ called it Paradise. And one day, we're told, in a magnificent reunion, they and we will be with the Lord forever.[1]

—Randy Alcorn

After Evie passed away and after our family went home, Josh and I managed to sleep for a few hours before the darkness of the night made way for morning. I woke up with Evie still resting on my chest. She was wrapped tightly in her soft pink blanket, but I had changed her into a new dress, a white christening gown our friend Laurie had kindly purchased for Evie to be buried in. I rewrapped the blanket and pulled the edges even tighter around her small frame, as if by doing so I could return a bit of heat back into her lifeless body. It was all I longed for, just a little more life for my little girl.

The nurses that morning busied themselves with the standard postpartum care. Some of them were kind; others were not. One especially rigid nurse saw my tears and told me, "It was just her time," like she expected her words to perk my spirits right up and erase all the painful memories of the night before. Her insensitivity triggered even more sobs.

Josh and I requested to be released from the hospital as soon as possible. We did not want to stay there any longer than necessary. But we also dreaded the moment where we would leave without our girl. How immensely unfair to leave the hospital without the baby we had just delivered.

As soon as I was cleared for release, the nurses instructed us to say our final goodbyes to our baby girl and left us alone. Josh and I gently placed Evie on the bed and snapped just a few more pictures of her. And then we stared at her tiny body lying there on that big bed and held each other, too paralyzed by our pain and enveloped by such a sense of surreality that we could not even cry.

The nurse came back with a plastic newborn cart. I rubbed some lavender baby lotion on my girl one last time, so that anyone who picked her up would know just by her smell that she was loved and cherished. I kissed her softly and then laid her in the plastic box. I stared as the nurse wheeled my baby girl out of the room. It all felt so strange, so absurd.

Josh left soon after to get the car from the parking garage, and for the first time, I was alone in the room where my daughter had died less than ten hours before. You might think that I sat in that room and bawled my eyeballs out over what had just happened and the life I was now expected to live without my baby. But I just sat there, numb, waiting for someone to wheel me downstairs. It was as if my brain had reached its threshold of thoughts and events labeled "hard to process." I waited in silence, in disbelief, in shell-shocked survival mode.

Another nurse soon came in to wheel me down to the first floor. Because my room had been located in the back of the mother-baby unit, she wheeled me down the entirety of the long hallway, passing room after room of mothers with healthy babies. I could hear them, the newborn cries, and the soft soothing words from the new mamas. Their sounds mocked my empty arms. The tears pooled in my eyes, and my chin quivered. I muffled my sobs behind tightly pressed lips.

The hospital staff gave me a handmade memory box crafted by some dear volunteers. I held the box tightly on my lap as the nurse wheeled me down to the hospital lobby. My face was red and swollen from crying, and the people we passed in the hallway stared at me. I vacillated between wanting desperately to disappear and wanting to shake each one of them by the shoulders and violently scream, "I just had a baby, and she died. She *died*! Do you know what that feels like?!"

Eventually the nurse and I made it outside to where Josh was waiting. It was noticeably very uncharacteristically warm for November and annoyingly sunny. As I climbed into the passenger's side, I caught a glimpse of the back seat. The absence of an infant car seat taunted me.

"It feels strange to go home from the hospital with no baby," Josh commented forlornly.

"Strange is one word for it," I muttered.

We hardly spoke as we drove the twenty minutes home. The birth of our baby should have brought bright, happy changes into our world. Instead things remained oddly unchanged, oddly the same. It was just as my friend Holly described after arriving home following her son Benjamin's death: the distance we traveled felt like miles, and yet our displacement was zero. We were very much changed and yet very much the same. And it stabbed and stung in all the places where a newborn baby would have brought such welcome changes.

Josh and I pulled up into our driveway and saw Micah playing in the backyard with his grandparents who had taken him back home after Evie passed away. Josh and I stood in the driveway under the shade of the giant oak tree and held each other for a little while longer as we stood in the sunshine and watched our boy play. How we ached for his little sister.

After a few moments, I breathed out a deep sigh and then walked forward and pushed open the gate of our chain-link fence toward my son. Josh's mom motioned to Micah to turn around and see who was behind him. When Micah turned around and saw Josh and I approaching, his eyes grew wide with excitement, and his entire face lit up. His lips parted into a full-mouth grin. He stood on his tiptoes and spread his little arms wide and ran up to me, his blonde hair bobbing up and down in the golden sun.

I scooped him up, squeezed him, and then gave him one thousand kisses all over. He cupped his little hands around my face as if to say, "I'm so glad you're home, Mommy!" Everything was right in his world now that Mommy and Daddy were home.

Later that night, after tucking Micah into bed, Josh and I were sitting together on our own bed, reflecting on the events of the last twenty-four hours, and trying to piece each of our memories together to build an accurate representation of what we had just been through. We were in a moment of quiet introspection when Josh turned to me with a weak smile, eyes shimmering with joy behind a veil of tears.

"Sarah, you know what Micah did when we came home, when he saw us walk through the gate?"

"Yes," I replied, remembering my beloved boy and how excited he had been to see us.

"That's what Evie did when she saw Jesus …" Josh's voice broke and gave way to even more soft tears.

Tears filled my eyes too, blurring my vision. What an amazing picture of what it might have been for our daughter to enter into the kingdom of God! What a gift for God to give us the tiniest glimpse of what it might have been like for Evie to see her Savior face-to-face.

I am not sure if Evie felt her brokenness while she was here on earth, but the truth is that she was very broken. Her body did not operate as it should have, and the consequences were fatal. She was weak and feeble, and she struggled to breathe. She may have felt every single one of those things in a physically uncomfortable way. But all of that was undone when she entered into eternity.

When Evie entered heaven, she did not carry with her the least bit of sadness for the life or the loved ones she left behind. When Evie entered into heaven, everything about her broken body that stole her life on earth was left behind. Her soul—the inner person she had always been—was more healthy and glorious than we could imagine. When Evie entered into heaven, she was not missing out on anything. Instead she was exactly where God intended all of His beloved children to be from the very beginning—in His presence, in perfect communion, no longer separated by the chasm of sin.

It is so easy for me to view losing Evie from only my perspective. It is so easy to mourn the loss of my own dreams with my precious girl that I forget what life is like from her vantage point.

If, as a mother, all I truly want for my children is for them to be happy, healthy, and whole, isn't that what Evie has in heaven? In heaven, fear, mistreatment, or a broken heart never threaten her. In heaven, there is no need for tissues, Band-Aids, or antibiotics. What Evie has in heaven is perfection, peace, and a forever of only the best in the company of God the Father. What more could a mother ask for?

From my vantage point alone, Evie's death was painful. It violently and carelessly jerked the tablecloth out from underneath my perfectly set table, sending porcelain dishes and glass wine goblets clattering and shattering onto a bare hardwood floor. But from where she stood—from the eyes of her own sweet soul—Evie's death ushered her into peace and joy like none of us this side of heaven have ever known.

Losing Evie felt incredibly cruel—like the enemy won and like he was shaking his gold medal of triumph in my tear-stained face. But that is what it felt like; it is not what was true. What was true is that God loved Evie much more than I ever could. He did not cause her to die because He didn't love her or because He didn't love me. In reality, He loved both of us so much that He gave up His precious Son Jesus so we would both have a way to live forever. A holy and right perspective does not see her death as loss but rather the greatest gain.

As a believer committed to Christ, I always strive to align my thinking with the perspective the gospel provides, not the perspective of this world. Could it be that my desire for Evie to have life on earth was actually a desire for this world more than the next? Did I simply need surrendered eyes to see that what she had was actually the best?

Paul describes what it is like for us to attempt to have an accurate impression of heaven while we are here on earth. "For now we see only a reflection as in a mirror; then we shall see face to face. Now I know in part; then I shall know fully, even as I am fully known" (1 Corinthians 13:12).

It is so difficult to see the reflection of heaven accurately when my heart is so tainted by grief, loss, and the stains of sin. But therein lies what it means to have faith, what it means to believe when I cannot see, when my pain prevents me from seeing. It is a choice to believe that what Evie has now and what I will have one day is far better than what we would have experienced together on earth. Because even our best moments here are tainted by worry, stress, longing, or imperfection. But in heaven, we will know perfect peace together.

God was not unkind in taking Evie, although it certainly felt that way. Instead of unkindness though, He displayed a deep love and affection by allowing the loss of His own child to pave the way for mine to spend eternity in heaven. He is a good, good Father who offers in the next life the best that this life on earth never could, all through His own Son Jesus.

Broken

We live in a world where babies die and mamas go home with empty arms.

Beautiful

The babies in heaven are experiencing perfect peace and communion with the Father who loves them dearly, a Father who made that existence possible through the sacrifice of His own Son.

13

NOT FOR A MOMENT

Our task is not to decipher exactly how all of life's
pieces fit and what they all mean but to remain faithful
and obedient to God, who knows all mysteries. This is
the kind of faith that is pleasing to God—a faith that
is determined to trust Him when He has not answered
all the questions, when we have not heard the voice
from the whirlwind.[1]

—Nancy Guthrie

Evie's brief earthly life was celebrated ten days after she passed away.
After a beautiful graveside ceremony with our closest circle of family and
friends, hundreds gathered at a reception hall at the Norfolk Botanical
Gardens to celebrate our sweet girl's homegoing to heaven. My dear
friends coordinated Evie's service and left no detail untouched. There
were gorgeous decorations and mountains of delicious food. Josh, our
sister-in-law Lauren, and beloved family friend Ben lovingly performed
a few carefully chosen songs that meant so much to me during my
pregnancy with Evie. A precious friend read a special poem, an original
piece she wrote just for Evie. I was able to go up in front of the room
and share the truth that, although I missed Evie with everything inside

of me, I knew she was happy, whole, and safe and would never again be touched by the cruel watermark of sin imprinted on earth. And my father-in-law spoke over all of us the truth of an invisible world watching to see how God's beloved children will respond in times of crisis.

After the memorial service was over, our close circle of friends and family went back to the home of our friend Amy who served us dinner and allowed us to use her home as a place to unwind after such a busy and emotional day.

The day after Evie's memorial service was Sunday, and I was busy with church things, including a lovely service for our church's annual Sunday-before-Thanksgiving Friend Day Celebration. It was so special to have that day to celebrate not just friends in general, but the selfless way our friends had shown love to us since the start of our journey with Evie and particularly at her memorial service.

I cried plenty over those two days but felt a deep sense of contentment seeing how Evie's life was celebrated. She was gone but certainly not forgotten; the memorial service had been an eyewitness testimony to that fact. That weekend had been the perfect ending piece to an otherwise tumultuous story. But when I woke up on the following Monday morning, all the feelings of peace and comfort were gone. It was as if all the sweetness of the memories of Evie's life and the celebration of her life were dissolved into a vast ocean of reality. She was absent now and no longer held my main focus of attention.

I had spent every day since Evie's death putting together as many handmade touches for her memorial service as I could. I would never have the opportunity to plan birthday parties for her, so this memorial service was all I had. I busied myself making handmade ornaments for guests to take home for their Christmas trees and decorated little packages of tissues to place on each chair in the auditorium. I even baked a few dozen cupcakes. It was a true privilege.

And as it turns out, it was also a distraction. Because while I thought I was actually in the middle of deep grief, I still had the memorial service to hold onto, and that made me feel like a part of Evie was still alive. But on Monday morning, after the funeral and the memorial service and the special Sunday celebrating our dear friends was over, I felt the cold, cruel smack of reality. I would spend every single day for the rest of my life without my daughter. And it started with this one.

The irreversible finality of death wrapped its icy, gnarled hands around my tortured heart. Evie was gone. Forever. In this life anyway, which felt like the only one that really mattered. And I was powerless to reverse any of it, the way humans are powerless to reverse the destructive path of a hurricane.

Shortly after learning of Evie's diagnosis, I had connected online with another mother carrying a baby girl with a fatal diagnosis. Samantha lost her darling daughter Nora about six weeks before I lost Evie.

Samantha and I talked on the phone once after Nora had passed away but before Evie did. I asked Samantha what it was like to have your baby die. She told me that it felt like her daughter had been ripped away—cruelly and harshly ripped away. I believed her that it would hurt that much. I just didn't know how accurate the description would be.

I felt it at my gut, the disgusted sense that every ounce of my love for Evie had no real direction, a sort of love inertia with nowhere to channel its energy. And my brain had no idea how to process this intense loss, leaving me half aware that life was moving on and half stuck in a loop of the same thoughts, same memories, and same feelings.

On that Monday after Evie's memorial weekend, I made an attempt to find some remote level of normalcy by thrusting myself into familiar household cleaning routines. I started with the bathroom but did not make it very far. After only a few moments, I dropped my scrub brush and collapsed into a confused, hurt, weepy, weary puddle on the floor. There were a thousand different emotions pulsing through my body, all with the undercurrent of sad, lost, and confused. The only coherent string of words I could muster up to the Father was, *What now, God? What am I supposed to do now?*

In a way that only God can move, He moved. At that very moment as I was weeping on my bathroom floor, trying to make sense of a world where babies die—where *my* baby died—and where life seemed to irreverently continue despite searing loss, my ears tuned into the song that was quietly playing from my laptop. It was the song "Not for a Moment" by Meredith Andrews.

> After all You are constant
> After all You are only good
> After all You are sovereign
> Not for a moment will You forsake me.[2]

God did feel very quiet on that dark Monday. My soul felt forsaken. But in that sweet moment through that pointed song, He was so kind to tell me that He was there and that He was not going anywhere, even as my heart shattered like thin glass on concrete.

There are so many times in life when we can feel like God is silent, particularly the times when our heart is breaking the most. And in those times, we tend to turn toward God in anger, shaking our fists and accusing Him of turning His back on us when we need Him the most. But as my friend Sarah so wisely shared, sometimes when God feels most silent, it is because He is being a true friend to us and sitting with us in the quiet, the pain, and the grief, just as a good friend would.[3]

My heart had anticipated the death of my baby daughter from the twenty-week mark of my pregnancy. My grief existed within the framework of processing my impending loss while Evie still kicked, squirmed, and lived inside of me. I was grieving, yes, but I still had the bright spot of looking forward to the time when I would meet my sweet girl. And of course, there was always the tiny glimmer of hope found in wishing for the most impossible of miracles.

But starting on that Monday, I became acquainted with grief as it existed in my new reality. Now the grief came in an entirely different wave. Evie's death was final. Now it was just onward, pushing through this life as a wife and mother, minus one. My loss and this new identity left me groping the dark for anything familiar to grasp onto to help gain footing and traction. But everything had changed. Nothing about who I had been before looked or felt the same.

After Micah was born, a dear lady came by to bring us a meal. Josh and I were snuggled under a blanket on the couch, our sweet one-week-old son lying contentedly on my chest. The woman saw my tired eyes and told me not to worry. She told me that life would get back to normal soon. It would just be a new normal. Her words were sweet and encouraging at the time as I struggled to figure out how to do life as a new mom. And those words still rang true after the loss of Evie. In my post-Evie world, I had to find a new normal.

Grief was my constant companion in the months following Evie's death. They say ignorance is bliss, and I was no longer blissfully ignorant to the pain and suffering that this world can offer, even to someone with a heart fully dedicated to the Lord. I was desperate to know if I were doing this grief thing right and, if I were, why it hurt so much. Why did I struggle to focus on normal life tasks like vacuuming or eating breakfast? Was my testimony bringing glory to God even as I lay in bed far longer than I should while my toddler son played Peek-A-Boo Barn on my iPhone for the ten thousandth time?

Praise God that Scripture is filled with people who have been well acquainted with grief and sorrow and that God's Word displays both the harsh reality of living a life filled with grief and still praising the name of the Father through it all.

The Israelites were a group of people in Scripture who felt that God had forgotten and abandoned them. And while we maybe shouldn't really look to their example as an exclusive outline for how to behave when we feel like God has left us in our sorrow (I'm looking at you, person who decided it was a good idea to make and worship a golden calf while Moses was on the mountain talking to God), I think we can learn a lot by one thing they did right.

In Deuteronomy 6, Moses instructs the Israelites to erect a stone monument to remember what God had done for them. He told them not to forget the works of the Lord their God. Each time God's people looked on the stone monument, they were to remember a great thing God had done for them, a way He had provided for them in their time of need. When the Israelites felt abandoned or forgotten by God, they could look to these monuments as a visual reminder.

In a similar way, 1 Samuel 4 tells the story of the prophet Samuel building a monument of stone to commemorate the Israelite victory over the Philistine army. It was a battle they would not have won except that God stepped in and helped them achieve victory. Samuel called the monument he built Ebenezer, or "Stone of Help."

One of my favorite hymns is "Come Thou Fount of Every Blessing" written by eighteenth-century pastor Robert Robinson. The second verse of that hymn says, "Here I raise my Ebenezer, hither by Thy help I've come." While my seven-year-old self may have been confused as to why this hymn referenced the crotchety old man from Charles Dickens' *A Christmas Carol*, I know now that it refers to this stone monument, this visual reminder of the help God provided for the Israelites. They needed a physical reminder, something they could touch or look at from a distance, something visible to remind them of the help they received from the Father.

In times of deep grief and sorrow, when God feels quiet, it becomes important to have personal reminders of God's goodness and provision of those times when your sadness did not leave your soul feeling so dry and withered.

During the months of intense grief, it was all I could do to remember God's goodness to me. I tried to praise Him for answered prayers of our time with Evie, like how, because of the time of day she arrived, everyone we wanted to be in the room with us was available to come. Or how she had actually been born alive, something we were not certain would happen. And I had been able to enjoy the sweet moment that so many people had been praying for, the one where I was able to hold both of my babies close—Micah and Evie—two sweet hearts beating next to mine.

Life is full of confusing moments, of times when God's purpose or plan seems so out of reach. But we can trust that He is ever-present by reminding our hearts of where He has already provided and of the times when we heard His direction so very clearly.

My sweet friend Rory and I have never met face-to-face, but we have the wonderful privilege of being internet friends. Several years ago, Rory and her family felt very clearly called to become adoptive parents and began their journey to adopt from Ethiopia.

Although international adoptions take quite some time to process, this particular adoption process was even longer, stretched out over the course of three years. When Rory and her husband finally traveled to Ethiopia to meet their son, it became very clear that he was not meant for their family and that they would not be able to bring him home. Rory was heartbroken.

Deeply grieved but not in despair, Rory and her family felt led to pursue adoption in China. This time they were matched up with a precious little boy. They had seen his picture, were receiving updates on how he was doing, and even picked out a name for this little boy. Rory's girls began to refer to this sweet boy as their brother. But there was a horrible mix-up and a severe miscommunication between the Chinese government and the adoption agency, and this little boy went home to another family. Once again, after feeling so strongly called by God to pursue adoption, Rory and her family were unable to bring a child home.

As you can imagine, Rory was so confused. She and her husband felt so confident that God was leading their family down the path of adoption. Why then was God allowing these opportunities to fall through time and again? Had they heard wrong? Had they misunderstood their calling? Were they meant to pursue adoption elsewhere or stop the process altogether?

Once I asked Rory what she was thinking and feeling as these adoptions continued to fall through, and she said something I will never forget. She said during that time when God felt distant and even contradictory, she kept reminding herself of the last thing He told her. What God told Rory and her family was that they were to pursue adoption. He never told them it would be easy or a smooth ride, only that they were to move forward with the process.

So often when our circumstances are uncomfortable and confusing, we want God to step in and change them. When we feel we've made a wrong turn or wrong decision, we want God to come in with a declaration that we can quit, that He's sorry He made it so hard on us, and that we can go back to how things were before. But in those times, we don't need a change of circumstance, only to do what my friend Rory so wisely shared: remember what God told us last.

The last thing God told me in that dark season was that He was there for me. He never said my grief would be easy, quick, or nonexistent because I was a follower of Christ. He only told me that He would never leave me or forsake me.

God is not a God of confusion, but of peace, love, and clarity. Perhaps the reason He feels so silent at times is because He does not have anything new to tell us, only that He wants us to keep moving forward in the last thing He told us. He wants us to continue to recall His past care and supply for our needs. We should not repeat the poor example of the Israelites who accused God of being unloving and uncaring despite all of His provision to them during their desert wandering and in their years conquering other kingdoms on the way to the Promised Land. We too have been provided for in the desert. We just have to remember.

I am so happy to tell you as I sit typing this chapter that Rory and her family have brought not one but two beautiful sons home from China. Praise God.

And for me? God never forgot me, even in my grief and even though my deep grief caused me to feel like He did. I may have been navigating a sailboat in the dark of midnight in the middle of a torrential downpour, but He was the lighthouse on the shore. I may not have always seen it clearly, for the sheets of rain that blinded me, but He was always there and has always been there, providing, leading, guiding, and never, ever forsaking.

Broken

Life circumstances can make it feel as though God has forgotten, abandoned, or failed to provide for us.

Beautiful

When life feels hard and God feels silent, we can remember the wonderful things He has already done for us, remember what He has already spoken to our hearts, and allow those remembrances to carry us through.

14

KICKING AND SCREAMING

The time when there is nothing at all in your soul
except a cry for help may be just the time when God
can't give it: you are like the drowning man who can't
be helped because he clutches and grabs. Perhaps your
own reiterated cries deafen you to the voice you hoped
to hear.[1]

—C. S. Lewis

The cold winter months that followed Evie's death slowly gave way
to spring. In many ways, the weather outside personified what was
happening inside of my heart.

In the immediate months that followed Evie's death, my maternal
instincts ached for the baby girl I had lost. I could hardly bring myself
to think about having another baby; I wanted that one particular baby,
the one with the chubby cheeks, the soft pink lips, and the name that
meant "life." But as the months pressed on, my heart began to grow
warmer and warmer toward the idea of inviting another baby into our
family. By late May, I finally felt ready for my rainbow baby—ready for
another precious life after we had lost such a dear one.

Unfortunately my being ready to add another baby to our family meant that I was completely overtaken with the expectation that the Lord would bless me with another baby girl, a healthy one, and immediately. I wish I could tell you that after everything I had been through and after all the ways my faith had grown because of my hardship that I waited submissively on the Lord and prayed fervently for God's perfect timing and that bluebirds sang hymns on my bedroom windowsill every morning.

Not so much.

I was fine when the first month passed without a positive pregnancy test. I mean, it was only one measly month, and I was, after all, very spiritual and very patient. After the second month passed, I felt the sharp sting of disappointment. By the third month, my emotions hovered around livid. And by the fourth month? There are no eyewitnesses, but my pupils may have burst into burning flames when I realized, once again, there would be no baby that month.

One particular day during that fourth month, the weather was depressingly hot and sunny, as it always is in late summer where I live. It is the time in late summer when most of the population is quite ready for the heat to be over, and yet it just won't quit. And that is exactly how I felt on the inside as well. I was undeniably ready for the pain of my loss to be over and for the news of a sweet new life growing inside of me to be the cool drink of water to my dehydrated soul. But that month would be another time of drought, of unmet expectation, of disappointment in the worst way.

I was absolutely through with waiting and had no intention of hiding my disgruntled feelings from God. I stomped through my house with all the subtlety of an aggravated moose, spoke to my son and husband in as few syllables as possible, and slammed as many cabinets and doors and drawers as I could. Subconsciously I hoped that my very outward displays of dissatisfaction would cajole the God of the universe to throw up His hands and submit to my will. This is hardly a good strategy for a toddler; it is embarrassingly absurd for an adult woman.

But I felt like I deserved this gift. After everything I had gone through and how much glory I had given to the Lord through it all (#humble), a healthy baby felt like something the Lord owed me. I deserved this, and I deserved it exactly when I wanted it—which was right now, please and thank you very much.

Sometimes I wonder if Noah felt that way. Noah and his family resided on the ark God instructed him to build while a complete deluge flooded the entire earth for forty days. Once the rain stopped pouring from the sky, Noah waited another 150 days for the waters to recede. After this, God instructed Noah to send out a dove to see if the bird could find a dry place to land, but the dove returned to the ark because there was no dry ground.

Forty days later, the Lord instructed Noah to send the dove out again. This time, the bird returned with an olive branch to indicate the water was indeed receding, but there was still no dry land. I'm not sure if you've been keeping up with the math, but that is approximately a lot of days on a boat with a single window, an entire family, and more animals than I have ever wanted to smell in my entire life. Each time Noah looked out and realized they couldn't yet leave the boat, I wonder if he had a similar thought, "Lord, didn't I do enough? Wasn't it enough that I built this boat, put my family on it, and brought all these creatures onto it, just like You said? Can't we be done now?"

I wanted to be done.

What I know about God's plan, according to common platitudes, is that we are to always yield to God's perfect will and His perfect timing. It sounds so easy when you just say it with words. But living out this principle when the delay involves the continuation of a hard thing? Well, then it just becomes that much harder to trust that God's perfect will and His perfect timing are indeed perfect.

One afternoon, late that same summer, I had the audacity to hand two-year-old Micah his milk in a red plastic sippy cup instead of a blue one. For whatever reason, he could not cope with this unmet expectation and absolutely lost any and all inhibitions. He began screaming at the top of his lungs and writhing on the kitchen floor.

"Pweeeeeassse, bwue one!" he wailed. "Pweeeeeasssseee!"

Knowing that my acquiescence to Micah's request while he displayed that sort of behavior was not in the best interest for his character development or the legitimacy of my maternal authority,

I chose instead to kneel down in front of him, calmly instruct him to gain some self-control, and then ask Mommy nicely for what he wanted.

I stroked Micah's shoulder gently and waited for him to gain some control over both his volume level and his fountain of tears. And in that tender moment with my son, I felt the Lord speak to my heart. *Sarah, how many times have I done this with you?*

A knot caught in my throat, and my eyes welled up with tears. In that moment, I reflected on the last several months and how I was essentially acting the same toward God about giving me a baby as Micah was acting toward me about his sippy cup color preference. In that moment, I felt as if I had a bird's-eye view of my life. From my spot on the kitchen floor, watching my son heave with tears, trying to overcome his fit of frustration over not getting what he wanted, I saw all the times that I acted similarly with my heavenly Father. How many times in the recent weeks had I allowed my intense desire for a pregnancy blind me to the work the Lord might have been doing in my life? Micah had a drink of milk available, just within his grasp, but he refused to be content with that provision because it was not how he wanted it to look. Had I done something similar to God's provision in my life, ignoring all the wonderful things I had because of the one thing I did not have?

It is not my intention to oversimplify a very complex, infinite God. I don't want to pretend to know what He is thinking or dogmatically claim that He definitively interacts with us in this way. But I do wonder, just as I had to wait for Micah to calm his frenzy before I gave him what he asked for, does God the Father also wait to bestow blessings until we are not so desperate so that our happiness and contentment aren't attributed to the coveted thing but rather His provision and truly perfect timing?

It is true that my contentment cannot come from things, no matter how wonderful the things might be. My contentment needs to rest in the place of knowing that God will provide everything I need at precisely the right time, to allow me to live the exact life He intends for me to live.

Sometimes what is best for me is for the Lord to not give some things, just for the mystery of it all so I can live in the surrendered place where my unfulfilled desires in this life will point me to the happiness, hope, and contentment of the next. As Lysa Terkeurst says, "If we always have everything we long for in this world, we'll be numbed to the deeper and much more eternal longings of our heart."[3] A baby could never satisfy the part of my heart that was made to crave eternal restoration with my Creator. That sort of contentment comes from Christ alone.

Micah eventually calmed down about his sippy cup, and my heart eventually calmed down as well. I still wanted a baby desperately, but I knew the Lord would make provision for that desire in His own timing. I had to unfurl my angry fist into a placid, open hand, willing to receive as God chose to give. And if He chose not to give, well, I would learn to echo the apostle Paul's words of contentment no matter my state of being. I was already a mommy to one child here and one in heaven. I could be okay with that, and life could still be very, very good.

One afternoon in late October, I hung up the phone from a very unsettling phone call, one that left my mind and heart reeling. Micah had been in a particularly, shall we say, high-maintenance mood that day, and while he was finally in his bed for rest time, I was still working on coming down from his craziness myself. And to top it all off, I was anticipating the start of another month without a positive pregnancy report. I huffed and puffed and stomped all over the house while trying to remember where I'd hidden the chocolate.

Out of frustration and a desire to have at least one of my stressors lifted in that moment, I decided to just go ahead and take a pregnancy test. True my body would tell me sooner or later, but I wanted to know right then.

I hurried into the bathroom, opened the drawer where I kept the box of pregnancy tests, and grabbed one. Moments later, I stared down at the very thing my heart had longed for those last six months.

The test was positive. I was pregnant. And I was scared to death. Josh's birthday was only two days away, and I thought it would be really fun to surprise him with the news. But considering how uptight I felt, I just rushed out to where he was studying in our finished detached garage and shoved the white plastic strip bearing double pink lines right in his face.

"Look," I demanded. My tone was crusty and unfeeling, like dry toast.

Josh looked up at me and then down at the positive pregnancy test and smiled. "Yay," he said sweetly. "Are you excited?" he asked, fully knowing how desperately I had wanted this moment for months.

"No. I'm scared. And slightly annoyed. And worried." I was definitely a mixed bag of emotions, but they were mostly all the bad ones.

"Aw, babe, don't worry. This is good." Josh kissed me gently and went back to studying.

I turned on my heels and marched back in the house, completely miffed that I could not join in his sense of optimism and sweetly subdued celebration.

What was wrong with me? I had dreamed about this moment for months, and now that it was here, I was a mess! I am now certain that fear crept in immediately—fear that this baby would be taken too.

Later that day I started a journal for this new baby, this brand-new little heart beating right under mine.

Dear Baby,

Today I learned you were here, growing inside of me. After six long months of trying, you're here. It's quite a relief.

But it's also scary. I have interacted with and heard of women losing babies at almost every gestational age, at full-term, and even shortly after. And after what happened to your big sister … well, I'm kind of afraid to hope. I wish my only emotion right now was excitement. Instead it's anxiety.

I found this prayer from Lysa Terkeurst. I think it will help me through until you're safely at home. "God, in this minute I choose to rest with you. I will not let my mind go to the minutes that are coming. I will simply be in this moment and face it with peace."

You are loved, Baby, and so, so wanted.

It took much longer than I wanted to get pregnant with my rainbow baby, although I realize that many mamas wait much longer. But I felt like it would have been so much nicer for the Lord to just let me get pregnant really quickly so I could continue to grieve and heal from losing Evie, all the while knowing there was a sweet little seed of redemption sprouting inside of me. But that was the blue sippy cup I had been so monstrously crying for.

Perhaps my good Father could not allow His daughter to have that good gift until she calmed down, wiped her face, and decided that she would be okay whether or not she ever had another baby. Maybe she needed to get to the place where she truly felt that God—and life in general—were still worth living for, baby or not.

Broken

We do not always receive the things we want out of life in our own time and sometimes not at all.

Beautiful

God is working something beautiful within us while we wait for what our hearts long for, even if that is just a greater and deeper desire for Him.

15

THE BROKEN PITCHER

There's brokenness that's not about blame. There's brokenness that makes a canvas for God's light. There's brokenness that makes windows straight into souls. Brokenness happens in a soul so the power of God can happen in a soul.[1]

—Ann Voskamp

At the beginning of 2014, I entered the second trimester of my rainbow pregnancy. My heart felt light, hopeful, and optimistic. The previous year I felt intensely inseparable from my grief. But at the start of this New Year, I felt as though the hardest parts of grief had been broken through. I was finally beginning to feel the light and life on the other side.

But even with the presence of this new light and life inside, the newness and optimism simultaneously occupied a space of tension. There was the broken side of me, the part of my heart that still grieved and always would grieve that Evie would never live with me this side of heaven. And now there also existed this joy-filled, hopeful side, where I very much looked forward to inviting a new baby to the family and celebrating all the blessings this little one would be. I had one foot in the camp of loss and one in the camp of celebration. Reconciling their polar opposition and finding some middle resting ground for both camps felt like a grueling game of tug of war with my heart as the rope.

After losing her fourth daughter to a fatal condition shortly after birth, Angie Smith felt a similar tension, an acute sense of loss and brokenness combined with a desire to live her life well, to the glory of God. In an effort to bring healing and insight to this tension, she decided to follow through on the suggestion of a friend who had given her a porcelain pitcher. This friend suggested that Angie take the pitcher, break it, and piece it back together as a sort of object lesson of faith, an illustration of what it might mean to live as a broken vessel before the Father.

And so, Angie took the pitcher out onto her front porch and smashed it. Then she collected all the fragments of pottery and took them inside to attempt the reconstruction project. As Angie pieced the pitcher back together, bit by bit, and then stood back to gauge her progress, she reflected on what God spoke to her heart in those moments.

> The image of my life as a broken pitcher was beautiful to me, but at the same time, it was hard to look at all of the cracks … I was mad at the imperfections, years wasted, gaping holes where it should have been smooth.
>
> But my God, my ever-gracious God, was gentle yet convicting as He explained, "My dearest Angie, how do you think the world has seen me? If it wasn't for the cracks, I wouldn't seep out like I do."[2]

After reading this story, I felt inspired to follow Angie Smith's example and try my hand at this same soul-reflection project. And so one morning, while Micah and Josh were otherwise occupied, I stuck a white porcelain pitcher into a plastic grocery bag (at the wise suggestion of Angie Smith to ensure the pieces wouldn't fly all over my back porch) and smashed it down onto my back concrete steps. The vase landed with a single muffled crack. Just for good measure, I gave it a few more swift hits with a hammer. Satisfied with the damage done, I brought the bag back inside and, armed with a glue gun, unwrapped the porcelain pieces from their plastic covering.

I sat at the kitchen table and worked and glued and pieced the tiny fragments back together. And I prayed. I asked the Lord to help me see what it meant to live life as a broken vessel. What did it mean to live life and move forward with some very significant parts of my heart shattered? What did it mean to be sad but hopeful, broken yet beautiful?

I wrote a blog post to document this experience.

> As I glued I prayed. I asked for my heart to be open. I petitioned for those who are hurting. I asked for at least one thing I could share. And as I prayed and glued, God spoke quietly and subtly to my heart.
>
> At one point, I kind of got stuck. The pieces had all been making sense and going together well, and then I just got stuck. The problem was that I couldn't even remember what the pitcher looked like. I couldn't put anything together anymore because I had no vision. Then I remembered that I had taken a "before" picture and should just use that as my guide. As I looked back between the picture and my work, the Lord brought this verse to mind: "let us lay aside every weight and the sins that so easily ensnare us, and let us run with endurance the race that is set before us, looking unto Jesus, the author and finisher of our faith" (Hebrews 12:1–2).
>
> When we become discouraged about the broken parts of life and our sins and weights lay heavy on our hearts, all we need is to look to Jesus. He is our guide, the perfect picture of what our lives should look like. We

rebuild our brokenness by looking at the picture of the whole—Christ.

A little further in my pottery-rebuilding journey, I was getting really discouraged. The pitcher was just not looking like a pitcher. I was pretty sure I had some pieces backwards or maybe upside down, and I thought to myself, "Sheesh! This thing isn't going to look anything like it was before!"

This time, the Lord didn't give me a verse but a thought, "After God has broken us, are we even supposed to go back together the same way?"

After losing Evie, there isn't a chance in the world I will ever go back to the girl I was before. And in some ways, that's sad. But in many, many ways, it's really for the best. Losing Evie has made me more sensitive to the hurts of others, more compassionate, more willing to put myself in someone's shoes and see pain from their perspective, more aware of how motherhood is such a privilege and not a right and a long, painful road for many. God broke me when He took Evie, but much of that brokenness has made me more like Christ. He doesn't want me to go back together just as I was before; He wants to make me new.

A bit more gluing and piecing together and I was done with my masterpiece. I had to laugh as I stood back to admire my work. I chuckled to myself as I thought there is absolutely no way this thing could ever hold water. And also it was ugly! And that is when the Lord revealed to me the final thoughts from this object lesson: this pitcher will never again be beautiful and hold water; it can never again fulfill its purpose as a decorative item or a liquid-holding vessel. Not so with us as the broken vessel and Redeemer God as the builder. In His eyes, the cracks make us more beautiful, more useful. The very imperfections and hurts that make us want to hide make the Lord want to shine through. We are never too broken or our hearts too ugly to be used by Him. He promises to restore (Joel 2:25).

I think this will be my personal theme for the year 2014—the broken pitcher. 2013 was a year of grieving and trying to figure out how to do life without Evie. 2014, Lord willing, has some really big and wonderful things in store for my little family (Josh's new career, a healthy baby #3), but in many ways I still feel broken. And this brokenness is something I have to learn to live with. So I'd like to learn to embrace this brokenness as part of me and move forward with confidence. I want to search my heart for those little places that are still shaking with fear and lay them before the Throne of Grace. I am broken, but this year I don't want to be fearful of that brokenness. I want to see myself as this pitcher—marred with purpose by the One who expertly crafted all the parts of my life.

Broken and Beautiful.[3]

In Jeremiah 18, God instructed the prophet Jeremiah to go down to the house of the local potter and observe what he saw there. This was meant to be an illustration of God's relationship with Israel. The Lord God says, "Just as clay in the potter's hand, so you are in My hand."[4]

Imagine an earthy lump of clay on a potter's wheel. This lump of clay is a mound of potential, but it will be nothing without the skilled hands of the potter. The potter is the experienced artisan with the expert knowledge of how precisely to shape this mass into something useful and beautiful. As the wheel spins, the potter shapes the piece of clay with pressure and guidance from his hands, sometimes collapsing the entire project if the sides become too weak. With the end result in mind, the potter knows just how much pressure will be required to shape the mound of clay into the final product.

Similarly, Father God knows exactly what sort of vessel He wants us to be. He knows that the end result of our lives should be a life that looks the most like Christ and a life that brings Him the most glory. And sometimes in order to shape our character into what it ought to be, the Lord needs to apply pressure and pain in just the right areas and at just the right times. But ultimately it is for our good, to make us into the most beautiful person we can be, because God is ultimately more concerned with the development of our character than the ease of our comfort.

Before I lost Evie, I had never really suffered much in life. Oh sure, there were mild hardships, interpersonal stuff, and husband-and-wife fights over who would take out the trash, but life was relatively easy. Before I lost Evie, there had never been a situation in my life where having a solid sense of determination and resolve did not see me through.

A dear friend of mine suffered from chronic illness and depression. She told me one afternoon after Bible study that she had spent the last couple of days on the couch, unable to get up because of her intense pain and fatigue. And do you know what I told her essentially? Suck it up and get off the couch. To this day, the fact that thoughts like those were in my heart and I communicated them out loud to my hurting friend is just so shameful to me. I am forever sorry that those words came out of my mouth.

But that was pre-Evie. Post-Evie, after I had experienced my very own heart-wrenching situation that left me tired and fighting for any semblance of normalcy in my heart and my life, I guarantee you that I would have responded much differently. I would have hugged my friend and told her I was so sorry. I would have told her that I was sorry life was so hard for her right now and maybe offered to bring her dinner that night.

Later that day, I would have texted her a red heart emoji, just so she knew I was praying for her and thinking of her. I would have responded with more kindness, compassion, and love, much like the Savior responded to every broken heart He ever encountered on this earth. That is one thing Evie did for me. She made me better at loving others.

Moving through life as a broken vessel can be so hard. It can be hard to reconcile the fact that peace and discord, wholeness and pain, and joy and sorrow can all coexist within the same heart. It can also be so hard to trust that God knows exactly what He is doing when He allows our own vessels to become cracked and shattered to the point that they will never again look like the vessels they were before. But this is the reality of a world tainted by the fall.

The comforting part of this reality is that God knows our hearts. He is there for us, even in those moments where it all feels so mucky and muddled. And it is in those mucky and muddled times that we have the opportunity to reach our weary hands out and ask for more guidance, wisdom, and tenacity to lean on Him, even when we don't understand. We can trust God's good heart and trust that the pain we endure will ultimately be for our best good and the good of His forever kingdom. We can trust that our brokenness will allow us to better tune our ears to the brokenness of others so we can meet their needs from our own broken places and attempt to make things just a little more whole.

We don't live this life as a broken vessel in vain. We live this way because we can always remember the Savior God who poured Himself out as a drink offering before the Father, an offering that would forever pay for our sins. We can live broken knowing that our brokenness brings us closer to the heart of Jesus, develops the best in us, and allows us to empathize with others who are broken as well. And in doing so, we do the worthwhile work of mending hearts here on earth and forever pointing them to Jesus.

Broken

Life leaves us cracked and bleeding, broken and bruised.

Beautiful

When we allow Christ to shine through the cracks of our own broken hearts, we bring His message of love, hope, and wholeness to a hurting world.

16

WOULD YOU BE OK IF ...

Perhaps the most blessed element in this asking and getting from God lies in the strengthening of faith which comes when a definite request has been granted. What is more helpful and inspiring than a ringing testimony of what God has done?[1]

—Rosalind Goforth

I bubbled with excitement and anticipation the night before my twenty-week ultrasound with our rainbow baby, the same kind that comes on Christmas Eve from the wonder of what lies beneath the tree. And much like Christmas, this excitement and anticipation was exactly for the uncovering and discovering of something unknown and long awaited: the next day, we would find out the gender of our sweet rainbow baby.

But despite my great excitement, anticipating the events of the next day was not just pure, simple joy. This anticipation also held all the sickening dread of anticipating something awful. Given our history, there was a real possibility that the appointment the next day would not go well.

I had been here twice before, the night before the standard

twenty-week ultrasound, the one where you typically find out if the baby is a boy or a girl. And both times the night before had indeed felt like Christmas Eve, a childlike giddiness of anticipating Santa Claus and all the treasures he would bring. But each time had such drastically different results. The first time was an overflow of joy, love, excitement, and pride. And the second time? Oh, the second time. Pain, confusion, despair, sadness.

This was my predicament the night before we found out the gender of our rainbow baby. I so desperately wanted the moment to be special and redemptive. I craved that moment so badly I could almost taste it. And I wanted it to taste sweet and melt satisfyingly onto my tongue, like soft-serve ice cream. But I knew the moment also held the potential to be the ice cream cone splattered onto the sidewalk, complete with hot, disappointed tears and shattered expectations. The moment could potentially spike my already tender heart onto hard pavement and cause more bruises and lacerations than I could handle.

But the strange thing (and something I hesitate to admit) is that my main source of anxiety that night wasn't primarily the health of the baby. What gave me the most anxiety was the baby's gender. Not only did I want a strong and healthy rainbow baby, I wanted a strong, healthy, rainbow baby *girl*.

After Micah was born, I sort of assumed Josh and I would only have boys. I thought I would be the quintessential "boy mom"— baseball games, muddy jeans, and pet frogs stuffed into pockets. One boy meant all boys, and I was totally fine with that. But when we found out that Evie was a girl, I felt a part of me sparkle to life. Even though I knew she would not come home with us, I dabbled in girl world and bought pink outfits, soft pink blankets, and handcrafted shabby-chic floral headbands. And then my girl passed away, stolen and ripped from me in the most emotionally assaulting way. This time around, my heart was desperate for a baby girl who could stay. I felt like my heart would not heal completely without having the opportunity to dive back into the world of fluffy and pink, of mother and daughter. I wanted it. I *needed* it. This rainbow baby could not be a part of my redemption story without it.

I knew this was wrong. I knew this was absolutely the wrong way to approach the upcoming news. I mean, what if this baby were a boy? Would I love him less? Would I resent his gender? Would I treat him differently because he wasn't what I had hoped he would be? In an attempt to ease my anxieties I texted a dear friend.

> PLEASE PRAY FOR ME FOR TOMORROW ... I'M SO NERVOUS. I DON'T KNOW WHAT I'LL DO IF IT'S NOT A GIRL.

After a few moments, she texted back. She told me not to worry at all and assured me that I would get my baby girl one day, even if it were not this time with this pregnancy.

My heart sunk. Her words fell empty against the hope I had placed in what she would tell me, a deflating balloon I hoped would rise high. I know my kind friend meant her words to be filled with comfort and encouragement, but in that moment, they felt vacant. There was no guarantee her words would ever be true. Just like so many things in life—like birthing healthy babies or a marriage that lasts for a lifetime—there are no guarantees. This includes the gender of a baby. I wanted my friend to text me the impossible guarantee that all would be well and fulfilled to my exact specifications, but she could not provide that for me. No one could.

I texted back an insincere "thank you" and put down my phone. With tears in my eyes and the unsettled feeling still in my stomach, I finally turned to the Lord in all sincerity, my heart searching for stability from a rock that would not be shaken. *Lord, I want a girl so badly. I don't know what I'll do if this baby is a boy.*

And with all the kindness and compassion of our sweet Lord who knew what it was like to live broken and grieved, He spoke softly to my heart. It was one question, simple in its asking and yet profound in its conclusion. *Sarah, if this baby is a boy, will you still be okay?*

I was startled at the question. In a way, it felt accusatory. Of course I would be okay! How could this mother's heart truly consider otherwise?

Immediately my heart softened. Would I actually be dissatisfied with bringing a healthy baby home just because the baby was not a girl? Would I actually be unhappy that the Lord gave us a child simply because the baby came home wrapped in a blue blanket instead of a pink one? Certainly not. While birthing a rainbow baby the same gender as Evie would certainly bring a special level of healing, I would be okay—more than okay—to have another sweet son to mother.

There are a thousand ways I have lived out this expectation that somehow God owes me something. There have been a thousand times I expected God to bless me in a certain way, to grant me the allotted three wishes simply because I grabbed the right lamp and gave it good a rub. But the harrowing, humbling truth is that I deserve nothing from God except the death that my sinful depravity would earn me were it not for Jesus who paid the ultimate price to redeem my debt to the Father.

Too many times I think I deserve something because I have waited well, reacted well, or endured well. But the truth is, even my righteous and good words are filthy rags tainted by pride, selfishness, and all manner of sin. Even my best efforts fall devastatingly short, never good enough or righteous enough to bridge the gap between my ugly sin and Holy God.

In God's great graciousness and love for me, He made a way for my sin to no longer separate my soul from His. What I deserve is hell, and yet, through Jesus, God allows me the option of heaven. O praise Him! But what is especially sweet about our heavenly Father is that even though we do not deserve certain gifts or blessings from Him, He loves us so much that His heart truly delights to give us good things.

I had filled line after line in my prayer journal that year, petitioning the Lord to bless me with another baby girl. I had even prayed for her by name, the name I picked out long before she was even conceived. It is always okay to ask God to bless us with good things—with really special things. But we must hold them all with an open hand, realizing that God knows the end of our story and how to best fulfill our requests. That was the part about prayer that I had neglected to keep at the forefront of my heart and mind.

On February 14, 2014, I lay on the same ultrasound table I had eighteen months prior in the same room with the same ultrasound technician. Josh stood on my left side, holding my hand. In his other arm, he held Micah up high so our sweet boy could see the flat-screen monitor. His smile was wide as he anticipated knowing if he were getting a baby brother or a baby sister.

Immediately after the black-and-white image of our sweet baby came onto the screen, I took a deep breath and asked if the amniotic fluid levels looked normal. Sue told me, with a knowing smile, that there was a lot of great fluid surrounding our baby. I exhaled, long and slow.

Thank you, Jesus! I silently praised, tears pooling into the corners of my eyes.

And then Sue zoomed in on the screen, right to the parts that would tell us whether we were having a boy or a girl. She didn't tell us though. Instead she asked us what we thought we saw. Or rather what we didn't see.

I know there are so many stories of loss that aren't followed by a beautifully redeeming rainbow baby. I know there are a great many of you reading this book whose arms still ache for the feel of the small weight of redemption cradled close. I don't know why that is your story and this is mine, only that this is the story God chose to write for our family. My prayer echoes yours that one day soon you will carry and snuggle and kiss your own precious baby. Until then, I pray you can stay grounded in hope and truth.

On Valentine's Day 2014, God gave me the sweetest gift. With teary eyes and a heart overflowing with joy and hope and a deep sense of love from my heavenly Father, I texted our dearest family and friends these words after our twenty-week ultrasound:

> HEALTHY …
> BABY …
> GIRL <3

What a gracious gift. My heart knew it. I did not deserve this baby girl because I had lost one. Instead my heavenly Father chose to give this baby girl to me because He loves me and because, even more than good parents here on earth, He knows how to give good and lovely gifts to His beloved children. And this is what He chose to give to me.

I did not deserve a baby girl, just like I do not deserve the heaven that is so graciously offered to me through Jesus. And as I would soon come to know, I also did not deserve a life free of additional brokenness and pain. I only deserved to have a heart even more surrendered to the reality of a broken world and surrendered to the Savior who alone holds the ability to make all things new.

Broken

Our own desires for certain outcomes can cloud our perspective toward how and when God chooses to bless us and what He chooses to bless us with.

Beautiful

Our kindhearted God truly delights in giving good gifts to His children.

PART III

LOSING AGAIN

GOD'S TRUTH CAN SUSTAIN AGAIN

For the word of God is living and active, sharper than
any two-edged sword ...

—Hebrews 4:12

The world was still asleep the muggy, sticky summer night we welcomed
our sweet Jocelyn Evie into our family. She was plump and scrumptious
with a beautiful head of dark hair. There was absolutely zero learning
curve for her when it came to breastfeeding. She latched on right away
and began to drink long, full swallows, as if she had been waiting the
entire nine months for that first taste of mommy's milk. Josh and I
chuckled over her appetite.

   We stroked Joci's sweet face and marveled at her cheeks and how
they looked like Evie's, chubby and rosy. Along with our family, who
had mourned deeply with us over the loss of our first daughter, we
breathed deep sighs of thankfulness and relief for this healthy baby girl.
From her first moments, Jocelyn filled us with joy and a great feeling
of redemption. Her name means "joyful life," and she epitomized those
words from her very first breath.

After Evie passed away, the doctors informed us they were fairly certain that what happened was a completely unfortunate, random occurrence. Evie's collection of anomalies did not point toward any definitive diagnosis or genetically predictable reoccurrence. Feeling confident that our time of sorrow and loss was behind us, Josh and I were ready to move forward with our lives and with continuing to build our family. Essentially the spirit in our hearts was to turn our heels and run full speed ahead toward building our family, with hopes that we'd kick some dirt into the eyes of the enemy who thought he could keep our spirits down and despairing. With our sweet Evie-girl in our hearts and our brand-new Jocelyn in our arms, we walked toward what we hoped would be a life free of loss and instead filled with life.

In early January 2015, I slipped a positive pregnancy test over the keyboard where Josh was typing out an email. His eyes grew wide, and he laughed an excited laugh from the depths of his daddy heart that was so ready to love again. He decided to tell Micah right away that we were expecting another baby but told him to keep it a special secret. Our vault of a four-year-old kept the secret for exactly one week. He listed it off very matter-of-factly one afternoon while showing his Pappa some new things in his room.

"And I have this new Lego set, and we moved my matchbox cars over here, and now I have a new baby in Mommy's tummy."

And just like that, our secret was out.

At only five weeks along, it felt really early to announce my pregnancy and maybe even a little reckless. But we decided to just embrace it, and soon everyone we loved knew about this sweet fourth baby growing in my belly. And while it may have been a little reckless to tell everyone we knew about this baby before I had even been to the doctor, it was important to celebrate this baby's life as early as we could. Because nothing could have prepared our hearts for the heaviness that would accompany this pregnancy just a few short months later.

It was a drizzly day with raindrops falling lazily and unpredictably as the four of us made our way into the doctor's office that morning. I wanted the kids to be at the appointment to find out if their new sibling were a boy or a girl. I dressed Jocelyn in a cute pink sweater and matching grosgrain bow for "team girl," and Micah sported a light blue polo shirt, showing off his spirit for "team boy." And I wore white to show my true neutrality because I honestly was going to be completely satisfied either way. "As long as it's healthy," as they say. But my heart even knew how to love the unhealthy kind.

The ultrasound technician was named Katherine, and she bubbled with compliments over our two adorable kiddos as she prepped my belly and her equipment for the twenty-week scan. Josh's smile was wide, and he wiggled his eyebrows up and down when I glanced up at him from my place on the table. I chuckled and smiled as we waited for the black-and-white image to appear on the flat screen overhead. A few seconds later, we saw the grainy outline of our sweet little baby.

But the image was hauntingly too grainy.

I tilted my head and stared at the screen, trying to remember what Evie's ultrasound had looked like compared to Micah's and Jocelyn's. As I squinted my eyes and tried to refocus my gaze, my heart picked up pace ever so slightly. Something felt off. My stomach seized up as I weighed the possibility of what I had hoped would be impossible.

And then Katherine spoke up. "Sarah, how much water are you drinking?" she asked rather inquisitively. "There is hardly any amniotic fluid in here."

Katherine's words were innocent enough. But to me, her words were searing, as if the enemy himself were digging his fiery fingers into my heart. I could hardly speak.

"I ... I drink a lot of water," I finally stammered out. But the words had no strength behind them. They disappeared into the air like smoke from a smothered campfire.

"What's that?" Katherine asked, still scanning and her voice still upbeat. "We'll need to up your water intake, Sarah." She repeated herself, just for good measure.

"No, I am drinking enough water." I pushed the words out this time, forcing them through my rapidly crumbling hedge of hope.

Josh's eyes were already brimming with tears. He spoke up and stepped into the space I could not. "No, she actually drinks a lot of water. We've done this before …" Josh's voice broke.

Katherine looked at us in what I imagine was a combination of disbelief and the unwelcome realization that she would have to articulate to us some incredibly awful news. She scanned and talked, stammering over her words as she tried to communicate exactly what she was finding, all the results of the same thing that had plagued Evie: no bladder, small lungs, broken heart.

Josh leaned over the bed where I was laying and began to cry quietly. "I'm so sorry, babe, I'm so, so sorry …"

I wrapped my arm around his back and patted gently. I felt numb, too numb to even cry. Instead I shook my head and smirked. The cruel irony of this broken world enveloped me. *Of course! Of course I would have to do the most awful thing I have ever done again. Of course!*

Disbelief and disgust over the sin-curse of the world flooded my insides. It had already affected me so deeply. And now I was expected to willingly carry this load a second time?

Unbelievable.

After Katherine finished scanning and reported her findings to the doctor, the doctor came in with a more detailed summary. We were told, yet again, that we needed to transfer my care to the maternal-fetal medicine specialist, and yet again, our hopes for bringing this baby home were very, very grim.

Our little family walked out of that ultrasound room carrying the weight of suffering on our shoulders. Micah, Jocelyn, and I waited in the lobby while Josh brought the van around to pick us up. Micah cried big crocodile tears as I explained to him that this baby would not be able to come home with us.

"But I want this baby to come home with us!" he cried, big and loud.

My tears fell freely, and my chin quivered. "Me too, buddy. Me too."

It was the absolute truth. I did not care that people stared at our little trio as we waited in the lobby. Our tears were raw, sincere, and unabashed. Our baby was going to die; weeping was the only response our hearts could manage.

After we came home from that appointment, I knew I had to make phone calls to our family to tell them the news. I felt like I was delivering conscription notices to young soldiers, sending them to a war zone of certain death. It still fills me with an icy shudder to remember what my mom sounded like on the other line when I called her with the news.

She was expecting my call, knowing that we had our ultrasound scheduled that day. When she answered, her voice was desperate, as if her maternal intuition already knew.

"Is everything okay?" she asked, her words pleading for it to be so.

I tried hard to swallow the tears, to make my voice clear, strong, and sure. But how exactly can a mother do that when her baby is dying inside of her?

"No …" I choked out, my voice cracked and shaky.

"Oh, Sarah, no! No!! No, no, *no*!!"

It was all she could say. It was all any of us could say.

Our whole family gathered together later that evening for dinner, crowded into our tiny living room. In the midst of a situation every single one of us wished would never happen again, we found ourselves right at the epicenter, anticipating the loss of another baby, grandbaby, sibling, and cousin.

Although the image had been very grainy and unclear due to the lack of amniotic fluid to clearly transmit the sonar image, the ultrasound technician told us that she was pretty sure we were having a baby girl. I had originally planned to make a beautiful vanilla cake with either blue or pink sprinkles baked into the inside to reveal the baby's gender, but considering what we were now facing, I made a chocolate cake instead. We were walking into another pregnancy with a disastrous end. Chocolate felt necessary.

As I slid my knife against the richly frosted cake and served big, thick pieces, our sweet Micah began to sing "Happy Birthday" to our new baby. We all chimed in, our voices raised in pain and prayer. We were tearful as we braced ourselves for what the next several months would hold.

It was such a strange place to be, knowing what I would have to walk through again. The typical assumption in life is that previous experience makes for greater ease of that same experience the second time around. It is why the phrase "practice makes perfect" exists. Going through something a second or third time tends to be easier because you already have experience from which to draw. Your responses and behaviors those subsequent times are based on what you did the first time, and often it is a much smoother process. It seems natural then to wonder if it were easier to carry to term a baby with a fatal diagnosis a second time. Was it easier since I had already done it and knew what to expect? In short, I suppose the answer is yes. But the more complete answer is considerably more complicated than one word can afford.

To use the word *easier* to describe what it was like to carry a baby with a fatal diagnosis to term for the second time would be like asking someone with a second cancer diagnosis if the dreadful chemotherapy treatments were *easier* the second time around. A better word than *easier* might be *familiar*. This second time around, I had a clear sense of treading familiar ground where the pavement had already been laid. But I still had to walk every sickening step of the way.

Evie's diagnosis completely rocked my world and caused me to break new ground with the Lord. It forced me to reconfigure my understanding of this world where defective combinations of DNA strands cause babies to die. After learning of Evie's diagnosis, I felt like I had to fight for truth and to focus on the good rather than the negative feelings that pulled weightily on my heart.

But after this baby's diagnosis, it didn't feel as much that way. Instead I was able to call once again on the truths the Lord used to sustain my heart that first time around. I was still in the fighting ring but had faced this opponent before. It was still grueling, but I wasn't on the ground grappling with darkness and on the brink of losing. I was a bit more privy to the enemy's methods and had experiential insight as to how to protect myself from his chokehold. But make no mistake;

it was still a fight. And the familiarity of knowing what was to come was not always beneficial.

When I went into labor as a first-time mom, I knew it would hurt only because people told me it would. I had no sensory experience to draw from, no scale on which to rate the pain. But the second time, I knew. I feared labor the second time because I knew what to expect and exactly how intense the pain would be.

In the same way, the familiarity of having a fatally diagnosed baby a second time was not entirely beneficial. I knew all too well what it felt like to watch my child die in my arms, the depth of helplessness I felt as the breath emptied from her lungs. I knew what it was like to leave her shell at the hospital and climb into the car, the absence of a newborn car seat too loud to ignore. I knew it all too well. I knew what was coming. And that was the most dreadful part of all.

But what I praise God for more than anything is the fact that His Word is the same yesterday, today, and forever. His truth can sustain whether it is your first time walking through something or the thousandth time. His words never fail because they are active and living, and somehow the Holy Spirit knows how to bring to mind the truth you need in the exact moment you need it. I praise God that His truth can sustain always and that its power never fades away.

Because of Evie, my heart already knew how important it was to love my broken baby. I knew how crucial it was to acknowledge my love for her and live my days with her as wholly as I could while she was here—to give her all of me. Because of Evie, I already knew how important it was to pick out a beautiful name. So I knew I had be very careful and intentional with my name choice for this baby girl.

After a great deal of thought and prayer, Josh and I decided to name our newest little daughter Katherine Zoe. Katherine means pure, and Zoe means life, a perfectly pure and sweet name for our baby girl, another one destined for heaven far sooner than we would have chosen. And once again, that promise of her forever home carried all our hope for our tiny, broken, beautiful baby Kate.

Broken

The nature of our broken world is that we have to endure painfully impossible circumstances time and time again.

Beautiful

God's Word is the same forever, and His truths are capable of sustaining any heart through trials, no matter how many times those trials may come.

18

I AM NOT THE ONLY ONE

Suffering invites us to be radically human with one another, perhaps doing nothing more than reaching across the table, clasping hands, and crying together. We are afforded the chance to create a safe place for someone to mourn; nothing is needed but space, proximity, presence, empathy.[1]

—Jen Hatmaker

Although learning of Evie's fatal diagnosis in the summer of 2012 was incredibly difficult, my life at that point actually felt like it held adequate space to process and grieve that diagnosis. If my life during that time were a little nest, my grief was a tiny egg inside, and every day I was able to tend to it, to prepare for it, and to become acquainted with it, even if just a little bit. But where my life held the capacity to process the impossible situation with Evie, it felt completely the opposite with baby Kate.

When we learned of baby Kate's diagnosis in the spring of 2015, Micah was four years old, and Jocelyn was almost one. Josh and I were in the process of selling our home, building another one, and moving across town. Josh was in the thick of working full time and also in the midst of a job transition. Since our home at the time was outside of the forty-five-minute travel window for Josh to be able to fulfill his on-call requirements for his new job, any weekend that he was on call was spent entirely at the hospital, over one hour away. There were many weekends that summer where we did not see him at all. When it came to tending my grief, my life felt much less nurturing nest-like and a little more push-you-out-of-the-nest-you'd-better-learn-to-fly-like.

In many ways, the busyness was my saving grace. I did not have as much time to marinate in my sad situation as I had with Evie. And maybe that was good. I praise God that His truths were there to sustain me once again because I am not sure I would have been able to make the space or time to dive into the same level of truth-seeking or sacred discovery as I had previously. Whenever I had feelings of anxiety or worry, I was reminded of a truth I had leaned on once before.

Anytime I felt particularly overwhelmed with everything I was carrying, emotional and otherwise, I would remember Psalm 61:2, a desperate cry to lead me to the only stable rock. I also knew how to turn the praise and worship music up when my spirits and thoughts were dipping low. And I remembered how to thank God for what was already planned with this sweet baby, the story He had already lovingly written for her.

That is absolutely not to say life was easy or the impending death of my baby did not affect me in a deeply emotional way. What I mean to say is that life continued to move at such a fast pace, and I was so thankful for the ground that had already been laid three years before. Had that not been the reality and my life continued to move forward at that same frenzied pace, I am not sure I would have survived very well. Thank God for His mercies.

Evie's diagnosis seemed to not only rock our world, but the world of many people around us. Our situation came as a shock to friends, family, and our local church community. As a result, Josh and I both felt as though a spotlight was shining on us. We felt a strong sense of obligation and responsibility to do this suffering thing well, to live in a way that would showcase the sustaining love and grace of Jesus to everyone who looked on with teary eyes. But after baby Kate was diagnosed, I felt a very different sense of obligation and responsibility to the world.

In the few weeks before Kate's diagnosis in mid-May, our friends Billy and Holly birthed a beautiful baby boy named Benjamin Paul. Benjamin's body was afflicted with CHARGE syndrome, a complex combination of extensive physical and life-threatening issues. Benjamin's body was very broken, with severe heart defects among many other delicate anomalies. This precious baby boy was delivered in the cardiac intensive care unit of the Children's Hospital of Philadelphia where a team of the most knowledgeable and capable doctors in the field of neonatal heart conditions could serve him. Benjamin struggled to survive every day of his two and a half months of life before finally flying away to perfect peace and rest in Jesus. Billy and Holly were absolutely heartbroken to lose their beloved son and returned home with empty arms. Where everything should have changed, nothing did. Their lives were left with a cavernous void where a tiny baby boy should have filled it in larger-than-life ways.

Around that same time, the news was absolutely saturated with the atrocities of the war in Syria and the surrounding Middle Eastern countries. As images and video clips of maimed children and homes reduced to rubble filled my newsfeeds every day, my heart was deeply broken for the mothers in those places. My life was enveloped by impending loss and deep grief, but at least I could tuck my darling living babies into their beds safely every night without fear of explosions or violent intrusions. This was a luxury these poor mothers did not have. Parts of my life may have been a nightmare, but for those mothers, their entire existence was a nightmare. As one Syrian mother reported, "We're just living on the edge of life. We're always nervous, always afraid."[2] That horribly inescapable reality was not my own.

Where my suffering felt highlighted by a spotlight as I anticipated the loss of Evie, with Kate, I felt the unmistakable sense that I was not the only one in the world suffering in a dreadfully unique way. I felt much more attuned to the suffering around me, and that intonation seemed to quiet the feeling that I was enduring the world's worst hardship. To be clear, carrying a fatally diagnosed baby to term is incredibly devastating, but my heart was keenly aware that I was not the lone sufferer in a world of broken.

With Evie, I felt the presence of very isolating emotions, a sense that I alone was walking through something very difficult. These types of feelings are quite common when we endure difficult things. Often those feelings can cloud our view and prevent us from seeing life from the perspective of another and can hinder our ability to view another person's hardship as actual hardship compared to our own suffering. Even still, as we weep and grieve over something lost in our own lives, we have the capacity—as followers of Jesus and lovers of souls—to find an extra place in our own hurting hearts to extend love, grace, empathy, and compassion. In Christ there is no comparing of stories, no base competition of who has it worse. In Christ and in this sin-tainted world, there is only one weary body draping the arm of another weary body around their shoulders so they can both limp on together. In Christ, there is only pressing on together.

In the same way, there exists abundant goodness in the world for all of us to experience. When one person receives something good, that does not exempt another from receiving something good as well, even if it is a very similar good thing. And we have the capacity to rejoice greatly with each other and for each other because, in the body of Christ, we all work toward the same goal and are always on the same team. We should cheer for our teammates, our fellow laborers in Christ, and know there are abundant blessings and good things to go around because our kindhearted Father knows how to give us all good things from His storehouse of good, infinite, and eternal.

Scripture tells us in Ecclesiastes 3 that there is a time and a season for everything. This includes times to weep and mourn and also times to laugh and to dance. Paul says in Romans 12:15 that the mark of a true Christian is the ability to weep with those who weep and rejoice with those who rejoice. And I believe this weeping and rejoicing with others happens even in the midst of our own tears and our own feelings of great joy.

Certainly so much harder though than weeping alongside a fellow weeper and laughing alongside a fellow rejoicer are those times when we are called to rejoice with another while our own hearts grieve deeply.

About six weeks before my due date with baby Kate, my brother-in-law and sister-in-law asked if they could come over and bring ice cream and chat with us for a little while. Of course Josh and I said yes, and we spent a few hours together that evening laughing and eating way too much Ben and Jerry's salted caramel core ice cream.

As they stood up to leave, my brother-in-law appeared slightly uneasy. "Um, we have something to tell you guys," Jed said tentatively.

My eyes immediately darted to my sister-in-law, Lauren. Not too long before we had a conversation where she told me they were seriously considering moving back to her hometown in central Pennsylvania. I raised my eyebrows in anticipation of this sort of news.

"We just wanted to tell you," Jed started again, "that baby number two is on the way for us."

My heart instantly flooded with relief that they were not moving away. And then my next reaction was excitement. I recalled in the same conversation where Lauren told me that she and Jed might move that she had also mentioned their uncertainty about having more children. The newborn days with their severely colicky firstborn had been so wildly difficult that they were very hesitant to go through the newborn experience again. But the Lord surprised them with an unexpected pregnancy. And although Jed and Lauren were quite shocked, they were also very excited to add another baby to their family. And of course, we were very happy for them as well. But when I turned to look at my tenderhearted sister-in-law, her eyes were brimming with tears.

"I'm so sorry," she whispered as she hugged me close.

It was only then that I realized the juxtaposition of their surprise pregnancy against the unfortunate circumstance of my own.

We said our goodbyes, and Jed and Lauren headed for their car. I made sure to stand at the door and wave goodbye from inside the house as they pulled their car out of our steep driveway. I smiled at Jed and Lauren on the outside, and inside, my heart was genuinely happy for them and their growing family. I prayed for only good things for the little life budding inside of Lauren.

But after they left and my thoughts turned inward, I could not help but feel some familiar feelings, the same ones I felt when I saw the pregnant inmate at the doctor's office three years earlier in my pregnancy with Evie. *Really, God? They didn't even plan to have another baby! Why couldn't you just let them stick with their plan and let me keep my baby? Why do they get one that they weren't even expecting and I have to lose this one that we want so very much?*

Life is so much this way. Life is the ebb and flow of blessing mixed with loss and happiness mixed with sorrow. And these stories written for each one of us are the very stories that will make us most like the Author and Finisher of our faith, Jesus. So while having a baby may have been exactly what my brother-in-law and sister-in-law needed in their story, the very element that would continue to shape them closer and closer to the heart of Christ, so losing baby Kate is what needed to be written into my story for the very same reason. And that sovereign plan over all is what allowed me to rejoice over Jed and Lauren's baby while I wept over mine; I knew that particular circumstance was what God called good in their life, and my particular circumstance was what He called good in mine.

One week before baby Kate was born, we all gathered at my in-laws' home with Jed and Lauren to celebrate their son Eli's first birthday. After he smashed and ate his adorable birthday cake, Lauren took him in the bathroom to clean him up and change him. Eli came walking back out into the kitchen bearing a tiny T-shirt with a bold message: Big Brother. Everyone laughed, there were some tears of joy, and we all hugged Lauren and gave her belly an affectionate rub.

That day we celebrated life—new life, growing life. And this same group of family and friends that gathered with laughter and smiles that Sunday afternoon would gather together with tears and broken hearts before the week came to a close, to celebrate another life in a very different way.

Broken

The world does not evenly distribute hard and good things. Sometimes we have to watch others rejoice when we are feeling most broken.

Beautiful

Because of God's sovereign plan over our lives, we have the ability to weep and rejoice with others, even in the midst of our own weeping or rejoicing.

19

LOSING A SON

He was despised and rejected by men, a man of
sorrows and acquainted with grief; and as one from
whom men hide their faces He was despised, and we
esteemed Him not.

—Isaiah 53:3

As we neared the thirty-seven-week mark of my pregnancy with baby
Kate, I became increasingly more aware that this sweet girl might also
arrive early, just as Evie had. Evie's absolutely movie-worthy delivery
made me quite leery of how my birth story might go with baby Kate.
This time, because of our recent move, we were a bit farther from the
hospital. We were also farther from family, with two kids at home
who would need to be cared for when I went into labor. In addition
to the other medical complications surrounding my baby, there was
an extra measure of complication because baby Kate was in a breech
position, indicating that her bottom was down instead of the preferred
birthing position of head down. This meant her birth would be a
vaginal breech delivery, which the doctors warned me would require
a bit more attention and maneuvering technique during the birthing
process. This included the recommendation of an epidural anesthetic

to mitigate the pain involved with those breech delivery techniques. So considering how the final stages of the birth process sprung up quite unexpectedly with Evie, I pleaded to the Lord that He would show me very clearly when it was time to go to the hospital with baby Kate.

My friend Jenna texted me one morning about three weeks before my due date and specifically asked how she could pray for me. I texted her back.

PLEASE PRAY THAT I WILL KNOW EXACTLY WHEN
TO GO TO THE HOSPITAL.

She responded with a simple prayer asking the Lord for clear direction when the time came, and I knew she would continue to echo that prayer throughout the rest of my pregnancy. Even in the midst of the angst of anticipating the death of another one of my babies, it was comforting to know that my sweet friend was coming alongside of me, bringing this request before the Father. I tried to quiet my heart and mind and rest in however God would choose to answer that prayer, knowing that whatever He chose would ultimately be best.

One Thursday evening after dinner, just a few days after Jenna's text, I started to feel especially heavy and especially pregnant. I had been experiencing the same practice contractions that I had with Evie, the ones that were not supposed to be painful but again, because of the lack of amniotic fluid, they were. These contractions were becoming less easy to ignore. As I shimmied around the living room picking up the mess of toys from the day and scooting around boxes from our move to our new home just one week before, I wondered if this might be the beginning stages of active labor.

Lord, You have to show me …

I headed off early to bed, this request on repeat in my heart.

I woke up at around 2:30 a.m., feeling the pain of contractions a little more intensely than when I had gone to bed. I moved from my bed to the blue corduroy rocking chair in Micah's room and sat there as he slept. I held my belly and tried to pay very close attention to what my body was doing. The contractions were coming, although not without inconsistencies, which had been the same element that confused me during Evie's labor process. Finally after about forty-five minutes or so, I headed back to bed, my heart uneasy as to whether or not that was the right choice.

Lord, show me! I pleaded once again and tried to close my eyes and rest. But I only chased the idea of sleep. Rest felt impossible as I simultaneously tried not to feel anxious about what was going on inside of my body. And then suddenly it came. The contraction I had been waiting for came. It was sharp, deep, and so undeniably labor that I jolted up to a sitting position, waking Josh in the process.

He sat up quickly. "Are you ok?" he whispered through the dark.

"It's time to go," I told him definitively.

He nodded and got out of bed, but not without first leaning over for a tender hug. We both knew what was in our very near future.

Josh carried Micah out of his bed and buckled him into the car. I did the same for Jocelyn, and we headed for the hospital with our sleepy-eyed kids in tow. I made the middle-of-the-night phone calls to our families to tell them what was happening and told them to meet us at the hospital. The voices on the other end of the phone were sleepy and somber.

As we drove to the hospital, Josh and I discussed in hushed tones some details about how we would handle the day.

Micah overheard us. "Wait, baby Kate is coming today?" he inquired.

We nodded a quiet yes in response.

"Oh yes! I'm so excited!" he cheered from the back seat.

Josh and I exchanged glances with no words. There were no words.

"The baby is coming today, Micah, but she will not be staying with us for very long, remember?" Josh gently reminded him.

"Oh yeah, I remember. But I'm still excited to meet her!" was his cheerful reply.

"Me too, buddy," Josh said quietly.

We drove in the dark of the night and made it to the hospital a bit before 4:00 a.m. Josh dropped me off at the main entrance, and I was directed down the hall and up the elevator to the labor and delivery floor. I walked slowly, the contractions still coming and my body still progressing in the labor process, but I finally made it to the check-in desk.

The triage nurses took me back to a room and hooked me up to the fetal monitor after reporting that I was about five centimeters dilated. They were quite alarmed by the baby's slow heart rate, and it became obvious that they had neglected to check my chart. I had the sickening privilege of recounting every detail of my pregnancy and this baby's condition, including the complication of the breech position.

Finally, after the birthing team present that night was up to date on the details of my pregnancy, they felt ready to wheel me back to the delivery room. I scooted off the triage bed and onto the wheeled hospital bed they would use to transfer me down the hall. As soon as I made it onto that second bed, I was overcome with the deep and twisting pain of a transitional contraction. My labor had again gone turbo.

I made it to the second room right before the intensity of another contraction rocked my body, making it almost impossible to climb onto the delivery bed. With one determined motion, I flung my body onto the bed and then turned backward to kneel against the headrest just seconds before the fire of another contraction radiated through my body.

"If I'm going to get an epidural, someone better get in here fast!" I shouted.

Josh had watched my delivery process with the previous three babies. He also administers epidurals as a part of his anesthesia profession. He took one look at my physical state and knew the reality.

"Babe, it's too late for an epidural," he stated firmly. "This baby is coming right now!"

A nurse heard me yelling and came in to check me. She could feel the baby's bottom with her fingertips. She urgently called for the delivery team, and the room became an absolute storm of commotion, with me at the center yelling out in pain and frustration. The delivery doctor was trying to maneuver the baby out, bottom first, while I writhed and screamed.

"I can't do this! I can't do this!" I cried out.

Josh came behind the bed and placed hands, strong and sure, on my shoulders. "Babe, you're already doing it. You can do it!" he confidently assured me.

I felt so stuck at that point of labor. The other babies had been head down, and when the pushing time came, the process worked just as it should. But with the baby's bottom down and her body folded into a V-shape in the birth canal, my pushing felt woefully unproductive. I felt stuck. The baby felt stuck. I begged for a break, for the contractions to stop so I could just catch my breath.

The doctor decided that it would actually be beneficial for me to go ahead and take a break from pushing, and I breathed a huge sigh of relief, even if just for a moment. She maneuvered the baby into another position and instructed me to push, and with every last ounce of energy I had, I pushed. Baby Kate was born.

I cried with relief and thankfulness that the process was over. But as soon as they placed baby Kate on my chest, I was reminded of what we had known all along.

Baby Kate was so very tiny, a mere four pounds and fourteen ounces. Her body was fragile and small. But the hardest thing to see was not her size, but how she labored for breath right from the beginning. Her breaths were only shallow and staccato, like the kind that come after you've been crying really hard for a long time. My heart broke, and the grief hit me down deep. *My poor baby.*

"Oh hi, baby. Hi, baby girl," I said through tears and in between soft kisses. And then I remembered that we had not been absolutely certain that this baby was, in fact, a girl. I needed confirmation.

"It is a girl, right?" I asked the nurse who was up by the head of the bed.

She took a quick look at our sweet baby and then announced, "It's actually a boy!"

"What?!" I exclaimed, my tears now intermingled with laughter.

I looked up at Josh who was smiling too. *A boy. Our baby Kate had been a boy!*

Late one evening, as we drove home from a visit to my parents' house for dinner, Josh and I had a brief discussion about what we would name our baby if the baby turned out to be a boy. We had a total of about five ultrasounds for this baby. In four of the ultrasounds, the sonographers concluded they were fairly certain we were having a girl, and only one said there was a slight chance it might be a boy. We had not received one single definite conclusion as to our baby's gender with any of the ultrasounds.

Since we knew the baby would not live long, my maternal instincts would not let me ignore the small chance that this baby could be a boy, and I did not want to be unprepared. And so we decided on a good, strong name, and I made sure to pack a newborn boy outfit, just in case. I am so thankful I listened to the small voice inside because when the time came, I was ready.

Josh and I named our little surprise boy Charlie Alan, the namesake of two great men in our family, Charlie after Josh's grandfather, Grandpa Charlie, who passed away suddenly when Josh and I were in high school. He had larger-than-life smiles, big hugs, big generosity, and big stories. My favorite memory of Grandpa Charlie is the time he brought home chocolate milk from a local creamery and poured big glasses for all of us to enjoy. He poured the milk glasses almost to the brim, so full that we couldn't even pick up the cup without spilling and instead had to bring our lips to the glass to take sips. He was a good man.

Alan is after my dad, a good, hardworking man gifted in mechanics and who shows his love through service and dependability. If baby Charlie had lived, I know my dad would have spent hours outside with him on the trampoline, seeing just how much higher than the fence line they could jump, playing Wiffle ball, or wrestling around on the living room floor. Baby Charlie's name honors these two great men.

The nurses took Baby Charlie away from me for a while in an attempt to supplement his oxygen intake, which was dangerously low. After just a short time, one of the nurses came over and asked me very quietly if I wanted to simply hold my son because he was not doing well. My answer was, of course, a solemn yes.

We dressed baby Charlie in his green and cream jumpsuit, the one with a little fox embroidered on the front. We wrapped him in a soft white blanket, and then Micah and Jocelyn came in to see their new baby brother. Micah was so excited to learn he had a brother, and Joci kept pointing to him and grinning and saying, "Beebee!" They both snapped pictures with the disposable cameras my mom had brought for them, so proud of their new sibling.

After a little while, the rest of our family joined the five of us in the room. They admired our new baby boy and laughed at the surprise that he had been. Somewhere in the midst of the pictures and snuggles from family and friends, baby Charlie slipped into eternity. When he came back to my arms, the warmth from his little face had faded into a tepid coolness. He was gone. It had all happened so fast.

Part of me grieves deeply, a little angrily even, that it wasn't me holding baby Charlie when he passed away. I wish so much that I could have sung him into eternity, just as I had his big sister before him. I would have loved to know the exact moment he passed so I could be certain that he had been ushered into heaven from a place of deep affection. But it was not me who was holding him in that moment.

Every time that memory comes into my mind, I have to push aside the anger and jealousy toward whomever it was that was holding him. I have to remind myself that whoever was holding him at that time loved him deeply and that he went straight from the arms of someone who loved him dearly to Father God who does, even more so.

Friends and family stayed a little while longer and took turns holding our Charlie boy. But as the morning went on, they all went home to try to resume their days, Micah and Jocelyn each going home with a different grandparent.

Eventually Josh and I were alone with our baby boy. I spent the day in bed with Charlie, snuggling him and napping with him. I examined his tiny toes and memorized the outline of his nose and cheeks, trying to imprint on my heart forever just a fragment of what this little boy might have been.

Josh and I pushed to leave the hospital that same day. There is something especially unpleasant about staying in the hospital where your baby just died. After I was given the all-clear for discharge, Josh went to go get the car, and I was left alone to say goodbye to Charlie, except for the one nurse inside the room.

I hugged Charlie's tiny frame close to my face and buried my head into his middle. I sobbed the kind of sobs only a mother can as she grieves over the shell where her child had once been. My chest heaved, and my lungs gulped in air. I forgot how to breathe.

"I would have taken good care of you!" I moaned. "I promise I would have taken good care of you …"

I tenderly wrote out a little name card to leave in the baby cart where he would be placed. Charlie Alan: beloved son. Because he was.

The nurse watched on with tears in her eyes as I placed my son in the newborn hospital cart. I hated that she was there. How hard to let a stranger watch your wretchedly raw and anguished moments. I climbed into the wheelchair, and she wheeled me away from the baby I didn't even get a chance to know.

Josh and I did not speak on the way home from the hospital that sticky late summer evening. His eyes were fixed on the road in quiet reflection while mine were fixed outside the window staring, but focused on nothing in particular. Despite the silence, we both knew what the other one was thinking. There was hardly space to think of anything else.

As we drove, we crossed over an expansive bridge, one that we cross every time we head home from downtown. But this night, while we were freshly bleeding from the gruesome gouge in our hearts, the evening felt especially quiet and still, as if the sky and the water surrounding us were somehow paying homage to the little boy whose giggles would never be heard in our home.

As I stared out the driver's side window across the car from the passenger's seat, my unfocused gaze suddenly became very intently focused on what was happening all around us. The sun was sinking low and painting an unmistakably vivid pink-and-blue watercolor sunset across the sky. The pink hue was bright and deep, like ruby red grapefruit. And underneath was a line of indigo that faded into a beautifully rich and bright blue, like the waters of the Caribbean Sea. It was truly breathtaking. And it felt sacred. Because somewhere in the beauty and richness of this watercolor sky was the realization that each of these two colors represented something for me, something deeply loved and wanted and yet painfully absent. The sky was pink, and the sky was blue, for my girl and my boy in heaven.

Hot tears laced the lower rims of my eyes, and I turned my head quickly from the stunning view. The moment felt like holy, sacred ground that required the removal of shoes, and yet I was not quite ready for it, not ready for that level of worship while plunged into that level of pain. Even though my eyes turned away, a voice rose up from within my aching heart and whispered something I could not ignore. *It's pink and blue for your babies, Sarah. I have them. I have both of them.*

God may have watched one of His beloved children say goodbye to hers that night, a sullen, mournful goodbye that no mother should have to endure, let alone twice. But it was not a God of indifference and apathy that looked on. Not at all. The God who looked on that night was our God who is intimately acquainted with grief and suffering, who watched His own Son die on a cross to pay for the lives of the children whom He created and whom He dearly loves. He did not watch me as a cruel puppet master weaving ill will and torture into the story unfolding on the stage. Instead He watched as One who also weeps, as One whose heart is grieved for the way of this world, for the sin of this world. He watched as One who made a way, through Jesus, for all of it to be redeemed.

God the Father gave me such a gift that night. As we drove back home to continue our lives fresh with loss and unchanged where things should have changed very much, God saw us. God saw me. He saw my broken maternal heart, and something moved within Him to reach out in a divine way and tell me that it was all okay, that Evie and Charlie were okay, that they were more than okay. They were happy and whole and in the presence of the God who loved them and who loved me. They were safe in an eternity that was intended for all of us from the very beginning. They were okay. And because of that, however messy a journey it might be, I would be okay too.

Broken

The brokenness of this world is such that sometimes babies die and mothers have to say goodbye to their children much sooner than they would have ever hoped.

Beautiful

God Himself is acquainted with grief and knows what it is like to lose a Son, a Son He willingly gave to make a way for our salvation.

PART IV

LIVING, LOVING, PRESSING ON

SURRENDERED FIGHTER

You wake up every morning to fight the same demons
that left you so tired the night before, and that, my
love, is bravery.[1]

—Unknown

We chose not to have a burial and memorial service for baby Charlie.
Not that his life was in any way less important than Evie's or unworthy
of celebrating, but because our hearts absolutely could not handle
another burial and memorial service for another one of our beloved
children. Celebration services surrounding the death of a loved one
are often an outlet through which the family can grieve openly as one
step in the journey of healing, but the scars in our hearts that were still
healing from Evie's death had been freshly ripped open once more after
Charlie passed away. As a result, Josh and I felt too weary to endure
another service celebrating life when we were still so wounded by the
pain of death. And so it was with the hope in our hearts that our sweet
son was already experiencing a spectacular celebration of life as one of
the newest citizens of heaven that we chose not to move forward with
plans for a memorial or burial service.

This choice proved itself to be the right one because one week later, on the day when we would have most likely held services for our sweet Charlie-man, my Grandma Martin suffered a fatal stroke. A few days later, I packed Micah and Jocelyn up into our minivan, and we headed up to Pennsylvania to celebrate the life and the legacy my grandma left behind. Once again, my heart was overcome with the realization that even in the midst of my own deep grief, I was not the sole sufferer on the planet. I was still called to weep with all of those family members who felt most affected by the loss of my dear grandmother.

One afternoon, shortly after returning from the trip up north, my friend Lori texted me and asked if she could come over. She was one of my people, one of my tribe. She was one of the few with whom I could share my heart openly and without reserve, confident that she could receive my words with grace and understanding and leave me feeling loved, validated, and encouraged.

When Lori came, she brought a gift. I opened it and found four beautifully decorated Anthropologie mugs with swirling floral designs and a matching monogrammed initial for each one of my babies. What a meaningful treasure.

Lori and I sat down at my kitchen table with mugs full of freshly brewed coffee. She looked at me tenderly and with expectant eyes asked how I was doing, the way someone asks how you are doing when he or she really wants to know and are willing to wait for the answer.

I told Lori that I was okay and that I was doing all right. I explained how life felt like it didn't even pause for me to grieve Charlie in the way that it seemed to stand still after Evie. After Evie, my life had space to be still, like when you're all snowed in for a few days in winter. But after Charlie, life felt like what I imagine it felt like for the Israelites when they fled Egypt and left their homes behind. They didn't even have a chance to let yeast rise in the bread dough, let alone grieve the only home they had ever known. They just had to keep moving. And so did I.

Tears filled my eyes, and silence filled the space between us. I looked down at my mug and rubbed my thumb along the smooth porcelain.

Lori finally spoke. She told me I was so strong. She told me that what she admired most about how I handled the whole situation with baby Charlie is that I had taken every hardship that came my way with an attitude of acceptance and surrender. She said I hadn't taken one single aspect of all the unknowns and allowed them to twist me into anxiety: not his initial diagnosis, the fact that we didn't know his gender, or the prospect of potentially having a C-section because of his breech position. She told me that I faced all of these obstacles with an attitude of, "Okay, so now what do we do?" rather than fighting against any of it. She told me I was brave and that everyone watching me endure this a second time thought I was incredibly brave too.

The tears fell freely as I listened to her words. I looked down at my mug and squeaked out my truth in barely a whisper. "But I don't feel brave," I confessed meekly.

I definitely did not feel brave. Because where I should have felt peace, I felt sadness. Where I should have felt confidence, I felt fear. And where I should have felt acceptance in God's good plan, I felt a searing pain in my heart and a profound longing for it all to have been very, very different.

"But that's what brave is," she told me. "It is brave to keep going even when you don't feel like it. That's what brave really is."

I nodded in agreement, not yet fully convinced that I believed her. But as the weeks pressed on, I began to move toward recognizing the absolute truth of Lori's statement.

There is a scene in the Star Wars movie *Rogue One*. A few dozen rebel forces land on an Empire base on mission to steal the plans for the infamous Death Star so they can become familiar with its inner workings in the hopes of destroying it. This group of rebels is basically on a suicide mission, but they fight valiantly for the cause of freedom.

In one scene, a band of rebels uses the broken remains of their ship as cover from incoming fire from a group of Storm Troopers. If the rebels can make it through the barrage of laser fire to the control system and shut it down, that will allow them a small victory in this otherwise hopeless battle and allow another rebel troop in a different area to successfully access the Death Star blueprints. One of the rebels decides to brave the incoming fire and declares, "I'm going for it!" He makes it out only a few steps before the enemy guns him down.

One evening as Micah watched that scene, he asked, "Is that guy dead now?"

"Yes," I told him, "he was trying to be brave, and he got shot down."

Josh quickly corrected me. "He wasn't trying to be brave. He was brave. He tried to go for it, and that makes him brave."

He tried to go for it, and that makes him brave.

Brave doesn't mean the absence of uncertainty and fear, but rather moving forward despite those fears and uncertainties. Bravery is being one step ahead of what you are most afraid of, even if it is a tiny step. Bravery isn't having everything under control. It is waking up every day and making the choice to continue to move forward despite feeling an obvious lack of control over your circumstances. Bravery is trusting that everything God says is true, that the faith you claim holds fast, and that Jesus truly offers hope that one day all tears will be washed away. Bravery is surrender to the fight and determination to fight, even if it is a wearisome battle.

I think all too often we expect to *feel* brave. We expect to feel brave, confident, and strong and move forward with the certainty that we can and will emerge victorious on the other side. But bravery isn't a feeling. Like love, bravery is a choice. It is the choice to feel anything but confident, secure, or assured of a win and to move forward anyway. Bravery is waking up to face the same challenges you did the day before and not losing heart.

For those of us in Christ, this bravery comes from the confidence that we know this life is not the end and that all the hard things we endure here on earth will pale in comparison to the peace, joy, and reward we will experience in heaven with the Father. In 2 Corinthians 4:8–17, the apostle Paul writes,

> We are afflicted in every way but not crushed; we are perplexed but not in despair we are persecuted but not abandoned; we are struck down but not destroyed.

We always carry the death of Jesus in our body, so that the life of Jesus may also be displayed in our body ... therefore we do not give up. Even though our outer person is being destroyed, our inner person is being renewed every day. For our momentary and light affliction is producing in us an absolutely incomparable weight of glory.

Even Jesus Himself, who experienced the most excruciating death on the cross, endured it all because of what He knew the Father had waiting for Him. Hebrews 12:2 speaks of Jesus's future hope as motivation. "For the joy that was set before Him endured the cross, despising the shame, and is seated at the right hand of the throne of God."

In Christ, we know we can face each challenge in life with bravery because we are on the winning side. When Jesus rose from the grave, He defeated death. In Him, we have hope that even death is not the final victor. In Him, we have the hope of life after death, a life filled with greater things than we can ever imagine, and a life devoid of pain and suffering. We can be brave because we know the end of the story, the part where God Almighty throws Satan down into the depths of hell forever and reigns with all righteousness and power. We can be brave because ultimately, we win.

In her book *100 Days to Brave*, Annie F. Downs writes,

Brave people don't give up. Brave people don't quit. Brave people realize that we rejoice in our sufferings because it leads to perseverance and perseverance produces character, and ultimately, it brings us to the hope we have in Jesus. Hope is worth fighting for.[2]

We can hold our lives with open hands because we know God is working. We can be brave in the face of the most unimaginable suffering because God is working in us and through us to bring about the best possible end, even if that end simply means developing character more like Christ or a heart that craves heaven more than ever before. We can fight for hope knowing that God holds our present and our future in His hands and make the choice to be brave in the midst of that fight.

May we never forget that the same power that raised Jesus from the dead lives in us. The same power that defied logic, physics, and medicine when it brought the 3 trillion cells of Jesus's dead body back to fully functioning life lives within us. There is power in us to be braver than we ever thought possible and power within us to charge forward with confidence because the spirit of the living God is inside of us. His power has proven to be remarkably, utterly, overwhelmingly, incomparably strong.

Philippians 4:13 tells us we can do all things through Christ who strengthens us. People have quoted this again and again to hurting hearts to the point where its message has become glib and sometimes even unwelcome. Because how can we do this thing—this incredibly hard thing that God has placed in front of us? It is because He is all power, He is all hope, and He is all brave. We can surrender to Almighty God and fight knowing that He is our defense, now and forever.

After losing Charlie, I felt this sense that the enemy was trying to get me down. I felt like he was taking cheap shots at my already wounded mama-heart. I felt like he was trying very much to win. And I was so determined to not let him win. Armed with hope and the knowledge that the victorious Lord was leading me, I moved forward through the tears and pain, as best as I knew how. I moved forward in bravery knowing that brave isn't a feeling. It is a choice, and with the power of Almighty God behind me, I had the power to be braver than I ever thought possible.

Broken

There are so many difficult challenges in life that can wear us down, and we can feel as though we are not brave enough to face them.

Beautiful

Bravery is not the absence of fear but rather pushing forward despite that fear and pressing on with full hope, confidence, and expectation of the beautiful future offered to us through Jesus.

21

WHAT WILL YOU DO WITH THIS?

Therefore, my beloved brothers, be steadfast, immovable, always abounding in the work of the Lord, knowing that in the Lord your labor is not in vain.

—1 Corinthians 15:58

There was a good fistful of questions that set up camp inside my head after Charlie passed away. I wondered if Josh and I would ever be able to carry another healthy baby. I wondered exactly how I was supposed to live my days not steeped in the paranoia that any and all tragic horrors would come upon my little family. And I wondered very much what my life would be like, right then, had both Evie and Charlie lived and my home was bustling with a four-year-old, a three-year-old, a one-year-old, and a newborn. It would have been insane, for sure. But it also would have been amazing.

Amid all the questions, one question seemed to take up the most prominent space inside of my head, one question that would not let up or let go and only grew louder as I searched for the answer. I desperately sought the Lord's answer to this question: what am I supposed to do with this story? If God allowed this identical tragedy in my life with the intention of propelling me forward into a greater purpose for Him, I did not want to miss it. I did not want to be the one that got away.

During that time, the parable of the servants and the talents was seared into my heart. This story is one that Jesus told in Matthew 25 to illustrate the kingdom of heaven. In this story, three servants are each given a sum of money or talents. Before he leaves on a journey, the master over these servants gives the first servant five talents, another two, and the last, one. The first two servants invest their money well and double what they were given.

Upon his return, the two servants who increased what they were given came to the master and reported to him what they had done with their gifts. The master commended them saying, "Well *done,* good and faithful servant!"[2] But the interaction between the master and the third servant went down much differently.

> Then he who had received the one talent came and said, "Lord, I knew you to be a hard man, reaping where you have not sown, and gathering where you have not scattered seed. And I was afraid, and went and hid your talent in the ground. Look, there you have what is yours."[3]

The third servant feared his master, and so, instead of investing well and earning interest on what he was given, this servant buried his talents. And the master was not pleased.

I did not want to be counted foolish as that third servant had been. The Lord gave me this one story and this one life, and I wanted to invest it, to make it more, to make it bigger for the Lord who had entrusted it to me. And so day after day, I prayed for the Lord to show me how. I prayed that He would show me what the investment should look like, the one that would one day allow me to hear, "Well done."

Now when I say I prayed every day, it was actually more like pleading—like a very desperate pleading. The word *beg* comes to mind.

My whole being ached, and my insides burned for clear purpose and direction.

Since I already had a blog, online writing seemed to be the most obvious path to take. I began writing more frequently and submitting articles to a few different well-known online publications. I scoured the internet for opportunities to submit my writing and studied the already published articles on those sites in an attempt to tailor my writing to what I thought they might be interested in. I was determined to make it work.

But it didn't work. Time after time, my writing was not accepted. In many instances, I never even received a response email. I began to feel very discouraged, like I was banging my fists against a glass wall and yelling to the people on the other side, only to find that they were unable to hear me.

It seemed that all of my grief post-Charlie was channeled into this desire to make my story known, to get it out into the world for the sake of not feeling as though my hardship was a waste of tears and heartbreak. I wanted Charlie's life to count. I wanted my suffering to count. I wanted everything that I had been through to count. It was not a wrong motivation by any means, but maybe there was a misplaced value in thinking my story would only count if the world could know about it.

My story with both Evie and Charlie counted as something even if no one ever heard another word about it. In Christ, all of our suffering counts for His glory, even if it is for the sole purpose of enduring that suffering well for the crown of life promised in eternity for those who do so. There have certainly been believers devoted to the cause of Christ who have suffered in anonymity, still to the glory of the Father and still to the value of building their own treasures in heaven.

Adoniram Judson plays the leading role in one of the most compelling missionary stories I have ever heard. In 1812, Judson felt called to minister to the Burmese people in what is now Myanmar. Throughout his missionary career there, Adoniram Judson lost multiple wives and children to illness and disease and suffered a brutal and unjust imprisonment. He was tormented by severe depression and finally died from a lung disease while on board a ship back to London. From Adoniram's perspective, it seemed for a time that his suffering was useless, that all of his hard work yielded such little fruit. I am sure his own heart sometimes wondered if his missionary career had been worth all of the loss and heartache.

Adoniram Judson suffered considerable loss for the cause of Christ while he served in Burma, but the believers there still revere him to this day as the father of their faith, the one who brought the gospel to their land. The Lord placed a burning in Adoniram Judson's heart for a people half a world away, and he followed. Time and again, there were chances to be discouraged and to quit, but Adoniram Judson remained faithful. No doubt he was certain that this would all count one day when he stood before the Father, even if he lost sight of it himself sometimes along the way.

For those of us committed to living for the Father, we can be confident that as long as we are obedient in our hearts to the Lord, we can trust Him with the results of what that obedience will yield. The Lord is not in the business of numbers and results, but rather moldable and malleable hearts that will be committed to His cause and not abandon Him, even when things feel most discouraging. Our obedience to God alone counts as His kingdom's gain.

We can trust the Lord with our stories and trust that even the most painful parts will count for something. Christian singer-songwriter Jason Gray has a beautiful song entitled "Nothing Is Wasted."

> The hurt that broke your heart
> And left you trembling in the dark
> Feeling lost and alone
> Will tell you hope's a lie
> But what if every tear you cry
> Will seed the ground where joy will grow?
> And nothing is wasted, nothing is wasted
> In the hands of our Redeemer, nothing is wasted[4]

In the hands of our Redeemer, nothing is wasted. The most broken parts of our lives can yield fruit, even if that fruit does not come to full realization until we are face-to-face with the Father, bowing low before Him in worship, offering to Him the crowns we have earned for enduring life well here on earth. Every detail of our story counts for the God who wrote it, for the God who knows it, and for the God who knows the ending. Every detail counts for the God who collects all of our seen and unseen tears in a bottle and comforts our hearts in a way that only He can.

Still there remained a fire inside of me to make my story known in a way that was bigger than just my own heart and my own people. I prayed desperately for a way. Or if this were a misplaced desire, I prayed for the Lord to take it from me. Surely I could live with this story as just a special morsel in my relationship with the Father, a story where only the two of us knew all the intimate details. But the more I prayed and sought direction, the more intensely I felt that I was not supposed to keep this one quiet. Like the servants who chose to invest their talents for their master, I felt the same.

One evening I was alone in my kitchen, cleaning up the dinner dishes. Micah and Jocelyn were tucked soundly in their beds, and Josh was working out in the garage. Like so many nights before this one, my thoughts were centered on prayer, on seeking, on the same pleading words.

Father show me. Please show me.

I was standing in my kitchen, my back against the counter, holding a dish towel in one hand and my favorite deep skillet in another. Again, I pleaded.

Father, show me!

The answer that came was undeniable. What followed this time was not more silence or more wondering but a single, unmistakable word.

Podcast.

Now I am a very practical person who was raised in a very conservative Christian church. Before this night, if you would have asked me if God speaks audibly to His people in this day and age, I would probably have said no, He doesn't really do that anymore. I would have told you that He speaks more in promptings and impressions of the heart through His Holy Spirit, which I do very much believe to be true. But I am also very well acquainted as to what my own thoughts sound like in my own head. And let me tell you, this was different.

This was so clearly different and so clearly not my own voice in my own head that I had been so accustomed to hearing those last several months. In fact, the voice felt so unmistakably audible that I instinctively turned around to see if someone were behind me. Of course it was impossible, considering I was alone in my kitchen and leaning against the counter that backed up to a wall of cabinets. But the word was impossible to ignore. After months of seeking and praying, the Lord answered my heart longing with one luminous word, *podcast*.

Immediately I felt the wings of a thousand tiny butterflies in my stomach. This felt so big and intimidating. *Podcast?* Like *I* should start a podcast? How exactly was I supposed to do that?

That night, for the first time in my life, I opened the purple podcast app on my phone and began browsing around for other podcasts that were formatted in a similar way that I thought I could maybe sort of try to do as well. My heart was racing, and my mind was brimming with ideas for the possibilities.

A few moments later, Josh walked into the kitchen from the garage. "How do you start a podcast?" I blurted at him.

He looked at me with eyebrows raised but answered practically about how you probably could just Google a step-by-step tutorial. I told him about my radical idea, and he caught my vision. He leaned with me over the kitchen counter and talked me through what it might look like to start a podcast. As providence would have it, we actually already owned a good bit of sound recording equipment in our home, equipment that Josh had used to record music for fun with his brothers a thousand lifetimes ago.

That night I went to bed with tingles of excitement in my middle, ideas flurrying around my mind like snowflakes. Over the next few days, those snowflakes settled and allowed me to build something from the freshly fallen snow, something beautiful, fun, and brand new.

While I know that my story did not require a very public outlet like a podcast to have weight and meaning in God's kingdom, I am so grateful the Lord gave me that gift. I am thankful that He prompted my heart, however afraid, to use my story to do something that felt much bigger than myself. I am grateful for the life He breathed into a heart that had been so touched by death.

Early in the spring of 2016, I launched my podcast entitled *The Heart Lessons Podcast.* The name was inspired by the idea that God doesn't just create us, set our lives in motion, wipe His hands free of us, and leave us to stumble along and figure it all out for ourselves. Although it can certainly feel like that at times, I will be the first to admit. But what I think is so amazing about God is that He doesn't just plunk us into the world to grope around and hope we get it right. Instead He works in every one of our hearts, prompting us through our prayers, scripture reading, the words and encouragement of others, and a thousand other ways to lead us down the path He has created for us.

That is what heart lessons are to me: a collection of those pieces of wisdom God uses to gently steer us along our way. They are the adjustments on the steering wheel of life to keep our path steady and true. I am so deeply grateful that God does indeed lead His children in this way, so we can fully live out the purpose He uniquely wrote for each one of us.

Broken

The pain we endure in this life can often feel purposeless, and we can be overcome by darkness and conclude that it was all in vain.

Beautiful

The Lord gives purpose to our pain, and no part of our story is wasted in His all-knowing hands.

22

THE BINDING OF A BROKEN HEART

Motherhood is a privilege beyond words, something that could only be thought up by such an amazing Creator.[1]

—Franchesca Cox

It was such a privilege to use my new podcast as a platform from which to share my story and the stories of so many other wonderful women committed to living their life in a way that pleases the Lord. It also meant so much to me that the Lord gave me that project born from the lives of my two babies who were no longer on earth. In a way, that podcast is their legacy, one thing I have done with what they left behind. That opportunity has been such a point of healing for me.

But I longed for another type of healing, the kind that would feel like a very direct and unmistakable redemption after the loss of baby Charlie. My heart longed for another baby. And while it felt like a very mild craving compared to how my heart had been ravenous for another baby following Evie's death, it was still something I longed for in the deepest parts of my maternal soul.

Josh and I talked at length about adding another baby to our family. We chose to go through with an autopsy and genetic testing after Charlie passed away. After Evie, the doctors felt as though what happened was an isolated experience since there was no singular genetic root cause they could identify. But after Charlie, even though the autopsy and genetic tests were still inconclusive, the medical professionals told us it was likely we carried some sort of recessive genetic trait that caused these anomalies. Because of this, we were to assume that we carried a 25 percent chance each pregnancy of losing another baby in the same way.

But we did not want this to be the end of our story. We did not want to end our attempts at growing our family on such a tragic note. Despite our knowledge of the odds, Josh and I both felt peace about moving forward and trying one last time for a healthy baby. We had no assurance that everything would be okay, but even still, we moved forward with a tiny flicker of hope in our hearts.

On the morning of March 16, 2016, I sat at my kitchen table, the world still dark outside the kitchen windows. I sat quietly, feeling very still inside, the way the world feels still after freshly fallen snow and before a single footprint has broken the smooth, white surface. If I were pregnant, I would be able to find out that day. But maybe I didn't want to know. Perhaps it was better to not know. Knowing would likely lead to worry and anxiety over the health of this new little life. So I decided to simply sit in the stillness and in the wondering.

There was a song stuck in my head that morning, and I kept repeating the lyrics over and over to myself in that stillness. The words were from Kari Jobe's song, "I Am Not Alone." The second and third verses played loudly in my heart.

> In the midst of deep sorrow
> I see Your light is breaking through
> The dark of night will not overtake me
> I am pressing into you.

You're my strength, You're my defender
You're my refuge in the storm
Through these trials You've always been faithful
You bring healing to my soul[2]

The lyrics had been so true to me. The Lord had been faithful to fight my battles all along with both Evie and Charlie. I may have walked through fire, but the very fact that I was still standing and had hope in my soul was a testament to the fact that I absolutely did not do it on my own. But what about the "light breaking through" part? Or the "you bring healing to my soul" part? I wondered if the Lord were telling me something.

A few moments later, I cracked open my Bible. I was four years into trying to read my Bible through in one year (#overachiever #notevenclose). Even though my pace was embarrassingly slow, that morning's reading held exactly the words God intended for me in that moment. "Let us return to the Lord; for He has torn and He will heal, He has smitten, and will bind us up" (Hosea 6:1).

Tears welled up in my eyes. I ran upstairs and immediately grabbed the lone pregnancy test taking residence in the back of my bathroom cabinet. A few moments later, I knew the truth of what God was telling me.

I was pregnant.

I waited until Josh came home from work that evening to tell him face-to-face. He was happy but reserved. Understandably so. We decided to keep things quiet about this baby until we had more information regarding the baby's health, a decision that was a little easier considering that we had to work out some insurance details before I could have an appointment at the midwifery center where both Micah and Jocelyn had been born.

I was thirteen weeks pregnant by the time I had my first appointment. I went alone, accompanied only by the anxiety that seemed to plague me since first learning about this rainbow pregnancy.

The ultrasound went well, and everything about the baby measured on point as it should have for my suspected pregnancy timeline. My due date was projected for November 21, right before Thanksgiving. How appropriate.

With a shaky voice, I asked the doctor to measure the fluid to see if everything looked okay as far as those levels were concerned. I also asked him to take as close of a look at the tiny baby's kidneys as he possibly could.

"If something were off with the fluid or the kidneys, would you already be able to tell?" I asked this same question over and over again in varying forms.

From what the doctor could see, everything looked fine. He was patient and kind and assured me, even this early, that he would most likely already be able to tell if something were wrong. All evidence pointed to a healthy baby.

"Do you want to know the gender?" the doctor asked me.

"I think I already know," I replied with a smile. It was most definitely not my first time staring at one of those ultrasound screens.

It was a boy. We were getting another baby boy. And praise God, this one would be healthy.

That afternoon, we showed Micah and Jocelyn the ultrasound pictures and told them we were having another baby and that it was a boy. Micah hooted and hoorayed so loudly. He was so excited for a baby brother. He was also the one to call grandparents the next day and report our happy news.

My sixteen- and then twenty-week ultrasounds reported good things for this baby as well. We were more than ready to welcome this baby boy into our family.

But for the sake of honesty and transparency, I have to say this pregnancy was anything but blissful. I felt so much tension in trying to be hopeful and yet facing the reality of all the horrible outcomes I knew to be possible. Yes the oligohydramnios that had afflicted both Evie and Charlie had been ruled out. But what about the nightmare of a random stillbirth? Or placental abruption? Or the cord wrapping around the baby's neck? There were so many potential disastrous outcomes, and my heart worried about each one, it seemed.

I also saw it in Josh's eyes and heard it in his voice. "I don't know what I'll do if something happens to this baby," he confessed to me one night.

The thought sickened me. He was the strong one. If he broke down, where would that leave me? It was all we could do to hold onto hope and push back these worst-case scenarios that tormented our thoughts.

There wasn't a ton of overly spiritual praying happening during that pregnancy. In my weakest moments, all I could do was string together a prayer of desperation.

Please, God, please let everything be okay. I am not sure we will survive otherwise…

Friday, November 18 was a sunny fall morning. I woke up with the kids per usual, got them dressed and ready for the day, and threw in a load of laundry. I thought I noticed some very faint contractions and made a mental note of the time, just to see if any patterns would develop. About one hour later, as I was cooking and serving up breakfast, I noticed the contractions were a bit more noticeable. Still not painful, but undeniably present.

Considering my birth story with baby Charlie and the fact that I had two kids with me at home right then, I decided it would probably be the worst thing if my labor kicked in very quickly and then suddenly I was pushing a baby out on my kitchen floor while my toddler and kindergartner looked on. I called both my mom and mother-in-law to tell them what was happening. I added the detail that they did not need to rush, but if they could just come in the next couple of hours, it would probably be a good idea for me to not be alone.

They were both there within thirty minutes.

I called Josh and told him as well, and he was able to get off work and come home. Since his work was about forty-five minutes away, we thought it would be a good idea for him to be closer to home in the event that we had another rush-to-the-hospital sort of situation.

I labored throughout the day, steady but not too intense, and took a long soak in the tub before getting ready for my previously scheduled forty-week appointment. When we arrived, the midwife Jennifer noted that I was indeed in labor but not yet ready to be admitted. She advised me to go home and rest, with the positive assurance that this baby would be here within the next day or so.

Josh and I went back home, and although I was a bit discouraged that things were not moving faster, I was ready to take a nap and let my body do what it needed to. Josh and I gave Micah and Jocelyn lots of hugs and kisses before each went home with a different grandma, telling them that their new baby would be here very soon. I watched the cars turn from our street onto the main road before heading inside for a nap.

I woke up a couple of hours later with some considerably stronger contractions. I spent the next hour upstairs laboring on my hands and knees, moving into the positions that would allow my pelvis and cervix to open up and allow for a smooth birthing experience.

At about 6:30, I went downstairs, where Josh was eating some leftovers. I told him I thought I was really in labor and maybe it was time to call the midwife. When I called and talked to Jennifer, I reported to her that I had been laboring a while and that my body was beginning to shake and sweat with these latest contractions. She told me to come on in and they would be ready for me.

When we arrived at the hospital, I walked up to the birthing center so I could check in and start the twenty-minute fetal monitoring process. The nurse checked my cervix for progress and reported that I was almost seven centimeters dilated. Tears immediately sprang into my eyes. I chuckled and asked the nurse for a high five. It was such encouraging news! I was in very active labor with my fifth baby. It would not be long before this sweet little guy was in our arms.

It was about 7:00 p.m. when the midwife cleared me to enter the birthing tub. The water was so warm and allowed my heavy, contracting body to relax deeply. Each time a contraction came, I would lean over the tub and plant my face on the damp cloth Jennifer had draped over the edge. It felt so cool and refreshing against my hot, sweaty face. In between contractions, I was able to relax into the water and put my back right up against the tub jets. I can hardly say that the pain of the labor process is amazing, but for what it was, the warm water was pretty amazing.

At around the forty-five-minute mark, I felt the overwhelming sensation of the transition contractions, the ones that come right before the pushing stage. There are no words really to describe the depth of the aching, twisting, burning pain except to say that these contractions take over your entire body in the most animalistic and primal way, in a way that makes you moan deeply, gutturally, and quite involuntarily. The memories alone make me shudder.

After allowing me to endure a few of those incredibly painful contractions, Jennifer decided it was time to break my water. She told me that what I needed to do was throw one leg over the side of the tub so she could have access to and break the amniotic sac. I hurled my leg over the edge of the tub in what felt like the most immodest position I could possibly imagine, and Jennifer broke my water. Almost instantaneously I felt the immense and overwhelming urge to push.

I sunk back down into the water and pushed hard. Just a few intense moments later, Jennifer placed her hand in the water and guided our sweet baby boy up to the surface. The first thing I noticed was the size of his adorable, chunky cheeks. And also he was loud.

We laughed at how bothered he seemed by the whole bringing-him-into-the-world process that had just taken place. I tried to grab onto him, but he was so slippery and wet. With the help of Jennifer, the nurse, and my husband, I climbed out of the tub and onto the bed to snuggle my new little man.

All I kept saying over and over, both out loud and in my own head was, "I can't believe it's over! I can't believe it's over!" And maybe what I was trying to articulate but couldn't, with all of the commotion of birth, was that I couldn't believe the entire thing was over—the anxiety, the pregnancy, and the birth—and that my living, screaming, and healthy little boy was now in my arms.

Many months prior, Josh and I discussed names for our son. Josh liked one particular name that I did not care for, but I decided to try to think of names that were similar. So I typed the name "Silas" into the Google search bar to see what I could find out about its meaning.

All four of our other children have such strong meanings behind their names. Micah David is a strong family name after his daddy and paternal grandfather. Evie Caris means life and grace, so fitting for our heaven-bound baby girl. Jocelyn Evie means joyful life and is not only a testament to what her presence brings to us but is also a tribute to her big sister. And Charlie Alan is named after a patriarch from each side of our family. So I wanted to make sure this baby boy's name had strong meaning as well.

The name Silas came up time and time again as meaning "man of the woods" and having a Greek origin. But in Aramaic the name Silas means "ask." Not "to ask" or "asked God for," just "ask," like a command.

Josh and I felt quite strongly that we wanted to try one more time for a healthy baby. We felt prompted to ask, just one more time, for a redemption life for our little family. And God so graciously gave us what our hearts longed for.

So for our fifth baby, our third boy, we chose the name Silas Archer. Silas, meaning ask, and Archer, for the reference that those of us in Christ are to always aim for the mark, for the bull's-eye, for the center. Silas Archer, our double rainbow, our special answer to prayer, the binding for our broken hearts.

Our boy was born right before Thanksgiving. We spent Thanksgiving Day that year at home with our family of five, ate frozen chicken pot pie, and decorated for Christmas. Josh and I spent that night on the couch, snuggling our precious son, with the bright lights of the Christmas tree shining on all three of us. It was a sweet time, one that I am humbly grateful for. We lost a son, and in His kindness, the Lord gave us another one. Silas will never be a replacement for Charlie, but he was and will always remain a beautiful, redemptive answer to our prayers.

Broken

After experiencing loss, our hearts can grow weary and desperate in waiting for redemption.

Beautiful

God promises that we will see good things here on earth and that He will bind our broken hearts.

23

BELIEVING A LIE

Deception has many endless variations, which
Satan tailors to our natural bents. Like a seasoned
fisherman, he selects the lure that he knows is most
likely to attract his intended prey—the one we are
least likely to consider harmful. He does not care what
we believe, as long as we don't believe the Truth.[1]

—Nancy Leigh DeMoss

While the safe arrival of sweet baby Silas was redeeming in many good
ways, I had experienced a great deal of anxiety during my pregnancy
over how my spirit would fare if the outcome were not positive.
These feelings of anxiety seemed to resurrect some of the emotions
surrounding my previous losses, ones that I thought had been bottled
up and carefully placed on the shelved archives of my mind. Apparently
these anxious emotions had not been corked tightly enough, and many
of them spilled outside of their bottles throughout my pregnancy and
in Silas's early newborn days. Now puddled out onto the surface of my
life were some areas where I thought I had made great strides in healing,
but that apparently still needed my attention.

I thought I had it under control, this whole idea of trusting God with uncertainty, of praying in faith, believing He could do anything but accepting His will over all. But I itched and ached in a very uncomfortable way, like wearing a shirt with a very irritating tag. I wasn't sure what was wrong exactly or what was causing the most emotional discomfort, but I felt that discomfort prompting me to pray for something outside of what my own mind and own capacities could provide for themselves. I felt the Lord prompting me to pray for a mentor.

There were some really wonderful people surrounding me during my grieving process with both Evie and Charlie, friends and family members who would take the time to listen to me as I talked through whatever aspect of grief I needed to verbally process. But no one could get inside of my mind and carry the burden for me. That was up to me alone. And for some reason after Silas was born, I craved something more than just my own processes, logic, and the occasional heart-to-heart conversation with a friend to keep my mind focused on truth. I craved a person older and wiser in the faith who could peer into my life and help guide me with constructive direction and a huge covering of grace. And although my parents and parents-in-law were wonderfully emotionally supportive, I also felt the need to seek someone who did not have the same emotional attachment to Evie and Charlie as these wonderfully devoted grandparents did.

The Lord began to impress upon my heart an almost urgent need to seek a mentor. I felt as though, throughout my experiences with both babies, I had been clinging very tightly to a rope as it dangled above some very deep and very dangerous waters. As time progressed, my grip began to slip. And as my palms and fingers grew raw trying to hang on with everything I had, I wished someone would come alongside me and place their own hands on top of mine and help me to hang on. I began to feel that the self-talk of repeating God's truth to myself over and over was no longer adequate; I needed someone else to speak this truth into me and over me. I began to feel weak and needed someone with spiritual authority and experience who could be strong where I could not.

Just a few months after Silas was born, an announcement came from the church stage that the women's mentorship program was opening for registration. The program would last from January to June, and each woman seeking a mentor would be required to meet with her mentor a couple of times a month, in person or over the phone, and commit to maintaining the relationship with the goals of spiritual guidance and growth. I was flooded with emotions of thanks to the Lord who had heard my prayers. He knew how weak I had become over the years trying desperately to hold onto hope and truth on my own. And now He orchestrated this perfectly timed program so I could find exactly what my heart hungered for.

A couple of months later, I drove to the mentoring matchup meeting with tears in my eyes. The leaders of the Walk It Out mentoring program were so adamant in communicating how they spend days praying over the potential mentor/mentee matchups and feel very strongly that it is God who places the matches together. As I drove to that meeting, I prayed and prayed for the woman who would be my mentor. My prayer was that she would be able to carry the weight of what I would hand her, all the pain, sadness, and pile of emotion that I felt I could no longer carry alone. I prayed that she would be able to speak truth and life into the places inside of me still raw and pulsing with pain. I prayed that she would understand and that God would use her to meet me exactly where I was.

Two hours later, I was driving home, this time with tears streaming down my face and what felt like a pile of pebbles in my throat. I had been matched with a woman named Brenda, a tall, middle-aged woman with blonde hair and glasses. She had a kind smile. She told me she was a preschool director, and I imagined, by her gentle voice and friendly eyes, that she was very good at her job.

What brought me to tears was the way God had so directly answered my prayers for a woman who could understand. Brenda had an adult son with Down's syndrome. She herself had to walk the painful road of an unexpected and initially unwelcome pregnancy diagnosis and a motherhood journey that was everything she would have never written for herself. She understood what it meant to have prayers for healing unanswered and what it meant to live with the sliver of doubt that God was actually as good as He said He was. She had been there. And now she was here to help me.

Between January and June, Brenda and I would meet—usually over mugs of hot tea at Panera—and chat about life. She would ask me about my week and offered some really helpful support and encouragement on the front of actively mothering my three children at home. And of course, she would always gently push to talk about the children I had lost, and we would work through how it had changed my entire worldview. She was so understanding and patient with me as I processed my life with her.

One afternoon I was feeling really discouraged about prayer. This discouragement was triggered by a friend's Facebook post requesting prayer for her baby girl. Instead of feeling compelled to pray for her and her baby, I was overcome with cynicism. *Of course her baby will be fine. God only takes my babies.* The thought was so ugly and wrong. I knew it, but I didn't know how to fix it.

I texted Brenda and asked if we could talk about prayer the next time we met. I told her that I was having some feelings of cynicism toward the whole process of how God answers our prayers, specifically the ones for healing. She replied and said that we absolutely could have a discussion on prayer next time we met. And so we set a date to meet the following week.

One week later, I met Brenda at Panera. She seemed uncomfortable as soon as we sat down. It was as if she had something to say and was not exactly happy that she was the one who had to say it. We chatted a bit casually, and then she asked me to tell her a little more about what I had been feeling toward prayer. I told her about the cynicism, about the feelings that God answers everyone else's prayers for healing except mine and how it had left me feeling confused as to what to think and how to pray when someone else asks for healing.

Brenda looked at me from across the little two-person table, her mug of hot tea swirling little wisps of steam into the air between us. She stared straight into my eyes and then began to speak.

"Sarah," she said, "I think you are believing a lie from the enemy."

Her words arrested me a little bit. It's a pretty big accusation to tell someone you think she has believed a lie from the Prince of Lies himself. But I urged her to go on.

"Sarah, do you believe God is in control?" Brenda asked.

"Yes." I replied.

"Do you believe God numbers all of our days?"

"Yes."

"Do you believe God numbered all of Evie's and Charlie's days?"

"Yes."

"Then I think you are believing a lie from the enemy that your children should have lived longer than they did."

Cue the record scratch. Hadn't I already dealt with this? Wasn't Psalm 139, the psalm that talks about the Lord writing all of our days, the biggest part of my comfort with Evie? Hadn't I rested in His sovereign plan over the passing of both of my children? How could I have believed a lie?

After a few moments of processing though, I realized she was right. I had believed that lie. Because if I had believed the truth about the number of days that Evie and Charlie had lived, then I would not feel as though God cheated my children of time on earth or had cheated me of time on earth with them. But that was how I felt. It was very sobering to come face-to-face with my cynicism toward God's sovereignty, the same God who had so tenderly carried me through the hardest times in my life.

Psalm 139 had brought me so much comfort in processing the lives of both Evie and Charlie. Those verses were my blanket of assurance in a circumstance that otherwise did not afford much certainty. But somehow still, the cunning snake that he is, the enemy wriggled his way into even the truth that had been so comforting to me. He found a way to plant something toxic in my heart, camouflaged among those beautiful truths. And it remained there, undetected, until someone much wiser and outside of my own head sought to eradicate it.

The question the enemy posed in my own life was a question very much like the first question he presented to Eve in the garden of Eden at the beginning of time. He never told Eve explicitly that God wasn't to be trusted or that she needed to take matters into her own hands.

He simply asked her if she were sure. And it is within those three little words that we still fight a great many of our battles today.

Are you sure God can be trusted? Because if He can, why did your marriage fall to pieces? Are you sure God is kind? Because if He is, how could that person have betrayed you in that way? Are you sure God is good? Because there sure are a lot of bad people who seem to have much easier lives than you do. Are you *sure*?

I've heard it said once that the enemy does not have to convince us that God is wrong, only that He might not be right. And that makes total sense.

As followers of Christ, we have a pretty decent handle on what we know God's character to be. If the enemy's battle tactics consisted of barraging our minds with a list of traits about God that were explicitly false—that were a complete 180 degrees from what we know to be true about Him—then we would recognize those lies more easily. We would more easily identify his sneaky, sinister ways and put a stop to whatever lies he was feeding into our souls. But the enemy does not work that way.

The enemy of our hearts is cunning enough to know that he has to be subtle and sly. He plants little doubts in our minds that don't look like giant boulders barreling into the water, but more like teeny, tiny pebbles that send ripples into the waters of our lives. He doesn't always try and turn us 180 degrees from what we know to be true of God, only to knock us slightly off course. But that little nudge is sometimes all we need to start us thinking about God in ways we never thought we could. A few notches away from the center of its trajectory can cause a space shuttle to completely miss its landing target. So just a few notches away from what we know to be true of our God can steer us away from our place of confidence in Him.

After Brenda shared that emotionally awakening and deeply revealing piece of wisdom with me, I thanked her. She breathed a sigh of relief that I had taken it well, a reality that she was not sure would be the case. We took some time to verbally process all the shock I felt over that realization, and I walked away from that night feeling renewed in my view of God and His sovereignty over my life and the lives of my children who were now in His presence.

Seeking the Lord on our own is incredibly important to build our own faith muscles. But sometimes it takes the perspective of someone on the outside looking in to help steer us back on course and help to refocus our own gaze onto the Father.

Brenda and I may not have directly talked about prayer, but that simple identification of the lie I believed was everything I needed to begin viewing my relationship with the Lord from a different perspective. I am so thankful that when I was too weary of the fight and too weak to hold on in my own strength, there was another person there to hold me up, to lift my weary head, and to point my eyes in the right direction. As the writer of Ecclesiastes scribes, "Two are better than one, because they have a good reward for their toil. For if they fall, one will lift up his fellow. But woe to him who is alone when he falls and has not another to lift him up!"[2]

Broken

The Prince of Lies is always seeking ways to penetrate our hearts with anything that can cause us to doubt God's goodness and His sovereign plan over our lives.

Beautiful

We have tools with which to fight this crafty, strategic enemy. We have scripture to guide us and an entire body of fellow believers who can hold us up when our own legs grow too weary.

24

IT ALL COMES BACK
TO JESUS

This is all my hope and peace:
nothing but the blood of Jesus.
This is all my righteousness:
nothing but the blood of Jesus![1]

—Robert Lowry

A couple of weeks after we found out that our sweet Evie-girl would not be able to survive outside the womb, a friend gifted me with a book entitled *I Will Carry You* by Angie Smith. Angie is an amazing writer, speaker, and overall influencer in the world of Christ-centered women's ministry, but I will forever be indebted to her for how that particular book became a survival guide for anticipating the loss of my infant daughter.

Angie lost her fourth daughter, Audrey, in a very similar way to how we lost both Evie and Charlie. Audrey was diagnosed at twenty weeks with a fatal condition that the doctors were never able to identify. *I Will Carry You* tells the story of Angie's loss and her healing journey afterward in what she beautifully refers to as the sacred dance of grief and joy.

I pored over that book and hung on to every word. When Evie was first diagnosed, I was desperate to find anyone who could give me insight as to what this horrible journey would look like. I had such a deep appreciation for how Angie so vulnerably shared what her emotions were like during that time. But maybe even more so, I appreciated her sharing the very practical aspects about her experience and the questions I was so preoccupied with finding answers to. Certain questions burned in my heart: what would it be like to hold a dead baby? how long were we supposed to keep our daughter after she died? All of these questions were answered, even if just a little bit, in Angie's lovely book. And they were invaluable resources to my bleeding heart and whirlwind mind.

You can imagine then how it felt to meet Angie face-to-face a handful of years later when she was the keynote speaker at a local women's conference the spring after Silas was born. I stood in line, shaking with anticipation and holding back tears as I waited for my turn for Angie to sign my book. When I did get to meet her, Angie was so kind and patient as I eked out something that might have slightly resembled human verbal communication about how I had lost babies like hers and how much her book had helped me. I can for sure guarantee that whatever I half-whispered, half-cried to her that evening hardly did justice for what her writing meant to me. The words she wrote held life-giving impact. And words that she spoke that weekend from the stage were equally so, not for guiding me through my loss but for the healing journey afterward.

During the Saturday morning session of the two-day conference, Angie retold the story of when God instructed Abraham to sacrifice his only son, Isaac. Abraham obeyed God, even though the command seemed harsh and Abraham undoubtedly had questions. I'm sure Abraham questioned how God would keep the covenant He promised, how He would make Abraham the father of many nations if his firstborn were sacrificed as a burnt offering. But despite this and other valid questions, Abraham obeyed, believing in great faith that God would raise his son, Isaac, to life again or fulfill the promised covenant in some other way.

Scripture tells us that as Abraham laid Isaac over the altar they had built together, and as Abraham raised the knife above his son's chest to carry out the act of sacrifice, God commanded him to stop. And just over Abraham's shoulder, he noticed a ram whose horns had been caught in the bushes nearby. God instructed Abraham to kill the ram and sacrifice that ram instead of Isaac. God provided a substitute ram so Isaac did not have to die.

I know it had been God's plan since the beginning for Evie and Charlie to live the lives that they did. I know He had written it into His good plan for the world, and this was exactly what needed to happen to bring about the greatest good for His kingdom and the greatest good in my own heart. But still I wish so badly that just as there was for Isaac, there could have been a substitute ram for Evie and Charlie. I cannot even tell you how many times I daydreamed about the doctors announcing that all the parts they thought were missing were actually there and that these were miracle babies indeed. I wished so badly for the Lord to provide a sacrificial ram to substitute for the death of my babies, but He did not. What He did provide was ultimately better.

"Instead of a ram in a thicket, God provided for us a Lamb on a cross," Angie shared.

These words challenged my heart deeply. Because sometimes I get so distracted wishing for the ram in the thicket instead of focusing on the Lamb on the cross.

Living my life wishing that God had not taken Evie and Charlie is a poor waste of energy. I would have given almost anything to not have them taken away from me. But that was not God's plan. It seems like having a substitute ram would have been better, at least for me. But what God did by providing a Lamb is a much better, more complete, more hope-filled ending to the story.

Instead of saving my babies in this life, God saved them for eternity by the sacred work of Jesus on the cross. Out of His deep, deep love and desire for us, God sacrificed His own Son to pay the price for the sins of the world so we could all be in a relationship with Him, if we choose to believe. Evie and Charlie were saved, but not by a ram. They were saved by the spilled blood of God's precious Lamb.

Because of the Lamb that God provided, my babies are whole, happy, and complete. They know no pain and heartache, and their bodies are no longer broken. God provided ultimate healing for them when He provided the sacrifice of the spotless Lamb on the old rugged cross. But God not only provided healing for them by way of the cross, but healing and wholeness in my life as well.

Apart from Christ, when I think of living life without two of my precious children here on earth, I am filled with agony. A deep, dark agony that leads down the road to debilitating depression and a life shadowed with anger and hopelessness. Apart from Christ, what faith would I have in a God who allows babies to die?

But when I contrast that darkness to the assurance I have because of Christ, I am filled with hope and thankfulness. What Christ's love compelled Him to do was to sacrifice His life to open the door for me to spend eternity with both of my babies. The end here is not really the end. Certainly my hope and joy in being with Evie and Charlie is delayed until my own death brings me home to Jesus, but we will be together again in a perfect eternity. Jesus made a way to give us hope in this life because of the guarantee His death and resurrection gives us for the next.

Sometimes when the calendar rolls around to the anniversary of Evie's or Charlie's diagnosis days or when their birthdays come up and their absences feel acutely palpable, I feel their losses in a sharp, painful way. In moments like that, I often think of Paul's triumphant words in 1 Corinthians 15:55, "O Death, where is your sting?" and I will often think, *Here. It's right here inside of me.*

Nothing in my life hurts down to the depths like having my babies ripped from me and the thought of spending all of my life here without them. But even though it hurts deeply, the sting of it all is mitigated by the hope I have in Jesus, His redeeming work on the cross, and the eternal life it leads me to.

The same is true for you. Although there are a great many circumstances in this life where we will feel the keen sting of death and the far-reaching repercussions of a sin-stained world, I can think of no life circumstance where the cross will not bring hope. No matter how painful or complicated, there is no circumstance that cannot have hope breathed right to its very core by this statement: because of Christ, one day it will not be like this. The power of the cross has the final word over all of our suffering.

A few years ago, I was a leader at a teen youth winter retreat. I took time to reflect on what I was still struggling with over the loss of only Evie at that point. I wrote these words in my journal,

> *A danger sign of temptation is when we want the things of this world more than the will of God. Was Evie's life on this earth a worldly thing? I need to have the perspective that God loves Evie too. In His mind, she is where He wants all of His children to be. He didn't cause her to die because He didn't love her. He loved her so much that He gave Jesus so she could live forever. A holy perspective does not see her death as loss but rather as gain. The greatest gain.*

In God's eyes, because of how Christ made a way, there is no mourning in the death of those that love Him. Psalm 116:15 tells us that in God's eyes, the death of His saints is precious because in that moment they are restored to Him. This is not a fairy tale, but rather a true story that has given God's people hope to keep marching forward during the most difficult times throughout the ages. God longs to be reunited with us, and because of Jesus, we have provision for that level of restoration.

In the end, it still just blows my mind how everything—all the hope, peace, and endurance—keeps boiling down to this one simple truth: Jesus died to bring life, and heaven is real. Nothing else offers the blessed assurance that no matter what happens in this life, one day we will exist in wholeness, peace, and joy eternal. There is nothing that the hope of the cross of Christ cannot touch.

What we once knew—a life as broken people plagued by the

consequences of a sin-ridden world—will all be over, replaced fully by a beautiful eternity in the presence of our sweet, sweet Savior and Father God who loved us enough to create that beautiful redemption story. I won't pretend that I live my life with a perfect knowledge or understanding of God's plans. But I do live in daily confidence and expectation that my broken is beautiful to Him because it keeps me dependent on His provision and clinging to His promises. My broken is made beautiful because it keeps my eyes forever fixed on the One who makes all things new.

Purpose from loss, hope from despair, beauty from ashes.

Here in the power of Christ, I stand.

Broken

Our world is riddled with the pain of sin and the consequences of the fall manifested in all manner of death and brokenness.

Beautiful

There is no sorrow here on earth that is not absolutely redeemed by the work of Jesus's death and resurrection and the promise of a perfect eternity with Him.

CONCLUSION

IF YOU LET IT

One thing I know to be true is that this is not the end, and that the loss of my children does not define me unless I let it. Instead, you can reap blessing from loss, as you have the powerful ability to empathize with those who have walked the same road. Your words, your embrace, your prayers. Everything you have to offer is from the first hand experience of deep pain and sorrow and the hope that can follow. You have the ability to tell a story full of redemption.[1]

—Jordan Tate

At the beginning of 2016, as I began the process of launching the Heart Lessons podcast, I made a list of potential guests whose stories and life experiences I thought would be really valuable to share on the show. One person I had on that list was my friend, Jordan Tate. She very graciously accepted the invitation to record an interview with me.

During her interview, Jordan shared her story of carrying to term her daughter Ellie after receiving a fatal diagnosis at their twenty-week ultrasound. She talked about the heart-wrenching pain of losing Ellie shortly after birth, the hope and excitement after learning they were pregnant with their rainbow baby, and the devastation of learning their second baby girl, Elsie, had the same fatal diagnosis as her big sister before her. Less than two years after Ellie passed away, Baby Elsie passed away too. Jordan and her husband, Chris, were absolutely devastated.

Jordan's mama-heart ached for a baby so deeply after Elsie passed away, and the Lord was faithful to open the door for her and Chris to bring home a beautiful baby boy through the blessing of adoption. Jordan's story is heavy with heartache and loss, but it is a beautiful picture of how God does still, even after immense loss, give good things this side of heaven.

At the conclusion of the interview, I asked Jordan the question that is the heartbeat of the podcast: what heart lesson did God continue to bring to mind as you walked that very painful season? Jordan's response was something I still think about to this day.

What Jordan said was that she felt very strongly the impression that this hardship had the opportunity to break her, destroy her marriage, cause her to lose faith, and so many other negative possibilities. But these negative outcomes would only be manifest if she let them. She said her heart lesson throughout that time could be summed up in four small words: if you let it.

If you let it.

That piece of intention, of will, of motivation to transcend circumstances, is crucial. And maybe even more than crucial, it is everything. Without the realization that we must carry out these faith things in a very active, purposeful way, there is nothing. Without the realization of that action piece, we will forever see these bad circumstances as things that happened to us, the suffering victim of life's cruel tortures. But we do have a part to play. We can overcome, or we can succumb.

If you let it.

God trades beauty for ashes and brings beauty out of the most broken places within us, but only if we let it be so. The beauty that comes from brokenness is most certainly something that can be thwarted by bitterness, anger, and a sense of self-entitlement against anything uncomfortable. If you want beauty to come from your story, if you want the Lord to restore the years the locust has eaten, you have to make space in your heart for that restoration.

If you let it, difficult circumstances can drive you to become bitter. Or if you let it, difficult circumstances can be the fiery furnace by which the gold within you is refined. The choice is absolutely yours to make.

Allowing beauty to come from your brokenness is not something that will happen upon you. You will not exist in your sorrow and then catch a glimpse of yourself in the mirror and think, *Oh wow! There it is, the beautiful soul that emerged from my suffering!* No. That is not how it works. How it does work is with a daily, moment-to-moment fight for what you know to be true, noble, just, pure, lovely, and good. It is a purposeful renewal of your mind time after time to focus on God's truths rather than the sneers of the enemy telling you to give up, to lie down, to quit trying.

Scripture is filled with the truth of how the God who authored the universe can bring good out of every circumstance. But there is an unspoken element in every heart that has been made beautiful through the broken; the willingness to bow to God's will in a sweet surrender, to humbly lay down personal agendas, and to let the beauty shine through, however painful. As the beautiful old hymn says, "'Tis so sweet to trust in Jesus, just to take Him at His word, just to rest upon His promise, just to know, 'Thus saith the Lord.'"[2]

As you read these pages, take the truths of my story and apply them to what the Lord is doing in you and through you. Don't neglect the element of personal responsibility. Allow God to do His work within you. Take my friend Jordan's heart lesson and press it deeply into your own soul and know that your story can either make you better or turn you bitter, if you let it.

There is a choice, friend, and it is yours to make. And it is not a pretty, popular, or wildly attractive choice. We often think that surrendering our brokenness to the will of the Lord looks a lot like a valiant knight riding a brilliant white horse, wearing the strongest, most resilient armor and waving a sharpened sword, ready for whatever the enemy has for him. But in reality, surrendering our hearts and allowing our broken to be made beautiful looks decidedly more like a battered, battle-weary soldier reaching a shaking hand out to the commander of the army, and separating cracked lips just to whisper, "Follow. I want to follow You to victory. Help me to follow."

I pass the sacred torch—blazing with refining fire—to you now. And you can most certainly cross your arms, close your eyes, and turn your head the other way, determined to sit in your grief and allow your life to be defined by the broken. But might I gently remind you that one day we will all stand before the throne of the Jesus who lovingly and willingly died for the gruesome sins of the world, who died so that through His brokenness, my brokenness and your brokenness could be made whole.

And as you stand in the crowd watching soul after redeemed soul place his or her crowns humbly and thankfully before His throne, I do not want the pang of regret to follow you there. Because in that moment you will have eternal eyes to see how every single part of your brokenness has been worked into something that will forever and always remain beautiful.

Friend, let your broken be made beautiful.

In the precious name of Jesus, may it be so.

ACKNOWLEDGMENTS

To Josh: Thank you for funding my dream. Thank you for doing all the dishes and bathing all the kids so I could write in the evening. Thank you for not letting me quit. Thank you for being a constant encouragement and a positive and driving force. Thank you for always rolling your eyes at me when I told you I was quitting. Deep down, I knew I didn't really want to. Thanks for knowing me so well to know that too. Also thank you for being gracious about my lack of brain capacity while writing this manuscript.

> "You … complete … me" – Michael Scott to Jan
> Levinson (Sarah Rieke to Josh Rieke)

To Micah, Jocelyn, and Silas: This was a dream of mine for so long, something I believe God put in my heart shortly after Evie passed away. I want you to know some things about this book:

1. This is what can happen when you trust God's timing and guidance and also ask for the input of really wise people. (Otherwise I would have written a really bad, half-baked version of this book a couple of years ago … all the praise hands that it does not exist.)
2. Your daddy supported me every single step of the way.
3. This is my story of how God is so very real. You will have your own story to tell one day. My prayer is this book will help open your eyes to see His work in your own life too.

4. (This one is especially for my Jocelynny, but good for you boys to know too.) Girls can do really cool things they dreamed of *and* be a mommy. We don't have to choose. It might be tricky at times, but that is why you need good people. (See the rest of this Acknowledgments.) Also never choose a man who thinks your dreams are dumb or not as important as his. (See #2.) ** Hint: pick one like Daddy.

Also thank you to the three of you for being so flexible and understanding when Mommy had to write and you had to be quiet, stay overnight somewhere else, or hear me speak in half-sentences over the last fifteen months. My brain was … yeah. Writing takes a lot of mental energy. Thank you for being gracious, even though you probably didn't realize you were even being that for me. I love you one billion Minecraft diamond ores, thirteen and one thousand sparkly pink unicorn cupcakes, and a hundred million concrete mixers. What a gift to be your mama.

To Pete and Soula (my parents): Thank you for reading this over and over to help me make it better. Thank you for watching my kids and encouraging and loving me through this whole process. Thank you for all the tears, prayers, and encouragement for always. You both are the truest of blessings.

To Dave and Teresa (my parents-in-law): Thank you for also reading my manuscript over and over and combing through to make sure it reached maximum potential. Thank you for watching my kids. Thank you for answering all of my questions and contributing writing and not laughing at all of my drafts. Thank you for being such solid sounding boards.

To Rachelen: Goodness. What a blessing your proofreading was to this whole process. Not just to the manuscript, but to my heart. Thank you for checking in and encouraging me all along the way. So grateful.

To Mary: The cover. *The cover!* It could not be more perfect, and I could not love it more. Thank you for being patient with me and working with me. Thank you for creating such a beautiful cover image for the story that cost so much to live and to write. I love it.

To Cara, Ginger, Cori, Kristin, Brittany, Caitlin, Sarah, Holly, and Lexi: Thank you for reading this and endorsing it as well as encouraging me in the most uplifting way. You saved my heart from despair so many times. Haha. It's hard to trust your own opinion of your own writing because eventually it all looks the way Charlie Brown's teacher sounds (womp womp, womp womp). Thank you for telling me these words were worth the publishing process.

To Lauren: Thank you for writing such a lovely foreword and being the truest sort of friend. I hope you know how much your love and support have meant to me for so long. I aspire to listen to others' hearts the way you have always listened to mine.

To Sarah, Lauren, and Tabitha: Thank you for encouraging me every time I wanted to quit. Thank you for telling me this dream was worth pursuing. Thank you for telling me it wasn't just a pile of garbage words. You gave me life so many times in the most holy form, the perfect GIF. (Haha!)

To my lovely online and podcast community: Thank you for supporting the work the Lord has given me to do and for being a part of the story He's written for me. I can't thank you enough for sticking around for all of these days, weeks, months, and years.

To the team at Westbow Press: Thank you for allowing my dream to become a reality. Thank you for allowing those of us with things to say to say them. Thank you for being a vehicle for my voice, my story, and my obedience.

To Jennie Allen, Jen Hatmaker, Shauna Niequist, Annie F. Downs, Sophie Hudson, and all the beautiful and influential women

on social media who encourage writers to write no matter what publishing houses are telling them: Thank you! I owe much of my bravery in pursuit of this book to your encouraging words.

Father God, Sweet Jesus, Ever-present Spirit: This is my humble offering, my outpouring of love for all You've done for me. I hope You like it.

To Evie and Charlie: I hope you like the book Mommy wrote. It is so people know about how you helped me know Jesus better. I love you both so much. Until heaven, my sweet babies …

APPENDIX A

HOW TO FIND CHRIST

There are so many references in this book to the beautiful salvation that Christ offers to us through His redeeming work on the cross. My hope is that you know this salvation, that you have accepted Christ's redeeming work as your only way to eternity with the Father, and that the reality of this beautiful redemption has already begun to heal some of your most broken places. But if that is not the case and if you feel ready at this time to accept Christ's gift of salvation, it is as simple as lifting your voice in prayer with these words,

> *Dear Jesus, I believe in You. I believe that You came to this earth, died on the cross for my sins, and rose on the third day. I believe that You are alive in heaven with the Father and offer me the gift of eternal life. I ask for You to cleanse me from my sins, and I invite You right now to be the Lord of my life. Thank You for offering Yourself as atonement for my sins and making a way for me to spend eternity with You. Today I say "yes" to You. In Your Name, Amen.*

If you prayed and accepted the Lord as your Savior for the first time right now, I rejoice with you! I am praying all God's blessings on your life as you walk with Him for the rest of your days. Please reach out to me if there is anything I can do for you.

Much love from your sister in Christ <3

APPENDIX B

HOW DO WE KNOW BABIES GO TO HEAVEN?

By Dr. David Rieke (Evie's and Charlie's Pappa)

Anytime true believers encounter "the shadow of death," their first impulse is to find shelter in the hope of the Christian gospel and rightly so. This is never more true than in a time of heart-wrenching infant loss, but on this topic, the writers of scripture are very encouraging.

Tragically though, because Christians have proposed a variety of answers to the question of what happens to babies when they die, confusion often reigns, and many Christians have been left to live with a crushing sense of dread over the eternal destinies of their youngest loved ones.

Inadequate Answers

For centuries, the Catholic faithful were taught that, unless their infants were hurried into baptism before death, their babies might be forever consigned to Limbo—a hypothetical place outside heaven in which babies feel no pain but also experience no supernatural happiness. This tradition evolved out of the idea that if a baby's "original sin" (which he inherited from Adam) was not washed away by the ritual of baptism, then he could not go to heaven when he died. The doctrine of Limbo was never unanimously accepted in the Catholic denomination, and in more recent years, it has been largely downplayed, but all this speculation only served to increase the confusion on this topic in many Christian minds.

Strict Calvinists have sometimes supposed that all "elect" infants go to heaven when they die, but the non-elect go to hell (while other Calvinists suggest simply that *all* deceased infants are elect). And still other Bible teachers have suggested that the babies of Christian parents (or parents of a preferred sect) go to heaven, while the babies of unbelievers go to hell. For the most part, these proposals are well-intentioned and thoughtful, but they certainly seem to be somewhat neglectful of some very important biblical data.

An Excellent Case Study

Most casual discussions of this doctrine seem to begin with a reference to the great assurance given by King David in 2 Samuel 12:23 when he was in grief over the loss of his own infant son, "I shall go to him, but he shall not return to me." This is indeed an excellent scriptural argument for the celestial destiny of deceased babies, but some object to this conclusion by noting that this particular verse properly addresses only the deceased child of a *righteous* parent and that David could have been merely referring to joining his baby in the Jerusalem graveyard someday, not necessarily in heaven. On the other hand, most Bible readers find this latter view a bit far-fetched since David seemed to derive profound encouragement from the prospect of being someday reunited with his son under joyful circumstances.

In any case, it is evident that 2 Samuel 12:23 alone is not adequate for settling the question of every deceased child's eternal destiny. But this text by no means stands alone in this discussion. There are actually a good number of biblical texts that address this subject in substantial detail.

Since Babies Cannot Know Any of God's Rules, They Also Cannot Break Any of Them

We learn from scripture that all humans everywhere are sinners by nature and, if they live long enough and are healthy minded enough, by choice. Furthermore, we learn that every Christian convert, transformed as he is by the "renewing of the Holy Spirit" (Titus 3:5) still retains his sinful nature right up to the time of his death. Only at death is the convert perfected, and only at death is his sin nature—his lifelong predisposition toward sin—finally eradicated.

In this respect, the deceased convert and the deceased infant are on an identical footing, both dying with their sin nature very much intact. Because of this reality, any suggestion that the infant's sin nature disqualifies him from heaven would have to disqualify the Christian convert from heaven as well and for exactly the same reason.

Additionally we learn from Scripture that God does not always charge certain sins to a wayward person's account*—especially when the person in view has no understanding of God's wishes and expectations. This truth is expressly stated several times in the New Testament.

The apostle James says, "Therefore to him who *knows* to do good, and does not do it, to him it is sin" (James 4:17). In other words, sin is charged to a person's account when that person knows God's command and opts to disobey it anyway. All of us in this life fall short of God's glory all day, every day, often in ways we aren't even aware of, but virtually the entire focus of scripture is on those moral failures that we *are* aware of, "known sins." We all wonder at times if we have become overbusy, overanxious, or oversensitive or if we have overindulged, overvalued, overworked, overeaten, overslept, overstated, overspent, overlooked, overreacted, and so on. Surely we are in some way at this very moment falling short of God's preferences and pleasure, and we may not even know the nature or extent of our failure. This is why the issue of *known* sin is the focus of scripture.

Repentance is a major theme in scripture, but a person cannot repent of a sin he does not know he has committed. Sacrifices were a major theme in Old Testament times, but an Israelite could not offer a sacrifice for a sin he was not aware of. Confessing sin is critical for forgiveness, but a person cannot confess a sin he does not know he has committed. Restitution is an important part of righteous living, but a person cannot make restitution for a crime he is not aware of committing.

Sorrow (being sorry) is an essential component of repentance, but a person cannot feel sorry for a trespass he does not know he has committed. In fact, entire passages of the Mosaic law were devoted to "sins of ignorance" (sins people might commit without being aware of their faults) and how these sins should be addressed when the people involved finally became aware of their trespasses (Leviticus 4–5, Numbers 15).

All these biblical passages come to bear mightily on the subject of babies who leave this world without even once in their lives "knowing to do good and failing to do it." If it were possible, as some suppose, for a deceased infant to suddenly find himself in eternal misery and separation from God's grace, a theologian or ideologue might be able to explain the infant's presence there as the result of Adam's sin, God's election, heathen parenting, and so forth, but the baby himself would have no explanation at all for his miserable condition or for why God was associating him with those who rebelled against Him in life.

The greatest themes of inspired scripture—the love of God, justice, mercy, grace, redemption, and Calvary—would all be utterly indecipherable, even contradictory, to everything within the grasp of his awareness. Indeed when "the books were opened" and "the dead were judged out of those things written in the books according to their works" (Revelation 20:12–13), what precisely could be found written against this hypothetical sufferer who died in infancy?

Repentance, confession, restitution, sorrow for sin, and desire for forgiveness are irrelevant to one who has never known what it means to do good and then rebelled against that knowledge. To those who know what is good, sin is both possible and is justly charged to their account. But babies are not included among these.

Along these very same lines, Romans 4:15 says simply, "where no law is, there is no transgression." The point of this statement is beyond question. Surely there can be no violation of a rule that has never been laid down in the first place. The apostle's argument in this case is that the hundreds of laws Moses handed down to the Jewish people only ended up multiplying their violations of God's rules, thus increasing their need for a gracious gospel pardon. In the case of babies, of course, no rule-giving or rule-breaking is even remotely possible. Infancy, being utterly devoid of rules, is also utterly devoid of rule-breaking.

Similarly, Romans 5:13 states that "sin is not imputed when there is no law." This was written to raise and answer the question of why people were suffering the penalty for sin before Moses delivered his hundreds of commandments to humankind. (Answer: Because they inherited guilt from the rebellion of Adam who was functioning as the representative head of the entire human household when he rebelled.) Even though personal violations of *Mosaic* standards were not being charged to human accounts in the centuries before God delivered His rules to Moses, the universality of death proves that Adam's original violation of God's command was yet being charged to each and every person.

Of course babies have also inherited guilt from Adam's rebellion, but the general principle of personal guilt being "imputed" only to the person who violates God-given laws is worthy of special notice in any discussion regarding the innocence of babies who for all practical purposes have no law.**

Romans 7:8 contains the declaration, "For without the law sin was dead." What hold, therefore, could sin and guilt have on babies who live in an intellectual state of absolute isolation from any law of God? This verse essentially compels us to conclude that sin and guilt have no hold of any kind on infants.

The apostle Paul's own experience with sin is described in Romans 7:9, "For I was alive without the law once: but when the commandment came, sin revived, and I died." Since Moses' law existed for centuries before Paul was ever born, we are forced to wonder how he could possibly say that he was once alive without the law and how it ever came to pass that when the law "came" to him he died. This passage is often debated in theological circles, but most Bible readers have concluded that Paul was referring to his infancy here when he speaks of being alive without the law. Then when he reached the age of accountability—the first occasion in his life in which he knew God's wishes and yet defied them—his personal sin was charged to his account by God, and he "died" in some sense of personal guiltiness before God. If this represents Paul's true meaning, then this text is another convincing argument for the heavenly destiny of deceased infants who were themselves "alive without the law once" and taken to heaven in that state.

Jesus Strongly Hinted That Small Children Live in an Exceptional State of Saving Grace

According to Luke's gospel (18:15–17), there was a time when small children were brought to Jesus, presumably by their parents, so Jesus might pronounce a blessing on their lives. On this occasion, Jesus referred to the small children and said, "of such is the kingdom of God" (v.16) and "whoever shall not receive the kingdom of God as a little child shall by no means enter into it" (v.17).

With these words, Jesus set forth the little children as models for His kingdom and all those who replicate them as recipients of His kingdom. Most Bible readers find it hard to imagine that Jesus intended in this "teaching moment" to include in His kingdom the adult replicas of these little children while excluding the children themselves in His analogy.

On a similar occasion, according to Matthew 18:1–6, Jesus took a little child in His arms and appealed to the adults around Him to become "like little children" in order to enter His kingdom, and He appealed to them further to be as humble as the little one in His arms in order to be great in His kingdom.

Furthermore, in addition to these rather sensational statements of Jesus in verses one through four, Jesus went on to emphasize the special importance that all little children hold in His eyes, making kindness shown toward them tantamount to kindness shown toward Himself and warning that the corrupting of their young spirits would be regarded by Him as an infinite crime ("it were better for him that a millstone were hanged about his neck, and that he were drowned in the depth of the sea," v.6). Once again, it seems impossible to imagine that Jesus intended in this "teaching moment" to include in His kingdom the adult replicas of these little children while excluding the children themselves in these examples.

Theological Summary

While we do not have a verse in scripture that explicitly states that all babies go to heaven when they die, we do have biblical assurance that the sins charged to any individual's personal account are only imputed because that person is committing them in defiance of what God has taught them in Word or conscience. The infant, small child, or severely mentally disabled person cannot know God's rules, and since he must know them and then fail to do them before his failure to comply is counted against him by God as sin (James 4:17), he is safe from condemnation for his failures.

Children spend their earliest years in a mental-spiritual state in which there is no divine law and therefore no transgression (Romans 4:15) and no imputation of sin (Romans 5:13). They are truly alive without the law in this immature intellectual state (Romans 7:9), but in the absence of any law, sin is dead to them (Romans 7:8).

Furthermore, we have biblical assurances that little children hold a place of special privilege and mercy in the eyes of the Lord as models for entering His kingdom (Matthew 18:3; Luke 18:17). And we have a convincing case study of infant glorification in the story of David's baby from 2 Samuel 12:15–23.

Closing Thoughts: An Allegory from a Sanctified Imagination

Come for a brief visit to heaven with me in your own sanctified imagination. (I wish the visit were real and that it could be longer for us.) Imagine having an angelic tour guide leading us to the Savior's own dining room in which all His followers are seated around Him in the warmest atmosphere you have ever felt—warmer than you ever thought possible. And imagine this celestial guide pointing out various people and groups of people around the Lord's table.

Off to one side is a group of God's elite warriors who sacrificed so much of themselves in life, disentangling themselves from "the affairs of this life" in order to "please Him who had chosen them to be soldiers" (2 Timothy 2:4). How bravely they fought in their lives—some to the death! How wonderful they all are—beyond wonderful really—and so very happy! We wish we could be counted among them.

On this side, our angel guide points out to us, is a group of God's special givers. During their lifetimes, they just worked so hard and gave so much of themselves to Jesus and His loved ones, often serving quietly and without being noticed—tears of love in the midst of animosity, songs of praise in the night, cups of cold water in His name, and sometimes expensive perfumes in alabaster vessels. Like the soldiers in the other group, the faces of these faithful workers and givers are simply radiant with affection and joy.

But now another group at Jesus's table catches our attention, a less orderly group with a somewhat more youthful appearance than the soldiers and workers at the table. These are, the angel tells us, a very special group of God's children. They don't really have any "war memories" or "work memories" to revisit and celebrate in the presence of Jesus. They didn't exactly *do* anything in the Lord's service while they lived below. This is because they had no time to do anything. They were so young when they died. They were never particularly tested in life or displayed as examples for their peers to follow. They did, however, inspire some remarkable spiritual passion in the older saints around them who fought and labored so faithfully in their own lives below, and the Lord treasures that reality in His heart.

Our angel guide explains to us that the Lord has a very special fondness for these children because His default feeling for all humans is affection and romance. But when human beings participate in the rebellion against His kingdom, as they all do if they live long enough, His feelings toward them become mixed. He still has deep affection for them, but He also experiences offended holiness, insult, and wrath in His feelings for them. These feelings of offense are all forgotten when His children are justified, but the consequences of their lifestyles below, for good or bad, are forever marked by their incorruptible crowns and rewards or their lack of them—their everlasting "rank"—in His home.

The angel explains that all God's children acknowledge the higher and lower ranks of those around them here in heaven, never with envy or sorrow (as those feelings don't exist in heaven), but just with awareness and acceptance of His special favors on this one or that one.

But with these young ones, our angelic tour guide explains, have no rank, per se, and no thought of finding their place in the "pecking order" or hierarchy of God's family. They all are just utterly convinced that they are Jesus's special treasures. They all just innocently expect all Jesus's special favors all the time, and truth to tell, they usually get them. The older children in heaven and Jesus all know that the Savior was once offended by their lives below and that the offense Jesus once felt is all forgotten, but these young ones and the Lord Himself know that He has never been offended by them a day in His life. They move through the corridors and gardens of the Lord's estate with a unique lightness of spirit. They look at the Lord differently than the older ones do, with a certain innocent and joyful sparkle in their eyes.

Whenever they have their family gatherings, the angel explains, the Savior loves to have the young ones nearby. They talk with no sense of inhibition at all. The young ones can chatter like magpies, you know. And the way they look at Jesus, the angel says, is so endearing to Him.

And now our tour guide takes us back home, and our imaginary vision together has come to its end. We are never safe to assume things about our Lord or to put words in His mouth, but a Bible-taught imagination might be at least a little helpful on at least some occasions.

Far beyond these speculations, however, scripture gives us compelling reason to conclude that heaven will be populated with some who enjoy a special rank and relationship with the Lord because of their battles in life over the years and because of their faithful and grateful labor and love for Christ. And scripture also gives us compelling reason to conclude that heaven will be populated with a class of "little ones" who have a special relationship with the Lord because, in part, they are utterly unmindful of any heavenly rank as it might concern them and because their unsoiled consciences fit them to enjoy a special sort of romance with the Father—perhaps a paradise kind of romance, as if sin had never even entered the world.

NOTES

* Imputation is an accounting term, the biblical equivalent to the idea of God charging an asset of righteousness or a liability of sin to one's account. English translations of Scripture sometimes render imputation in familiar accounting terms: "counted to him," "accounted to him," "reckoned to him," "charged to him," and so forth. We find in scripture that Adam's sin is imputed to every person from the womb, that each believer's sins are imputed to Christ at conversion, and that the righteousness of Christ is imputed to each believer at conversion. Romans 5:13 ("sin is not imputed where there is no law") also indicates that a person's own innumerable offenses to God are not charged against his account unless God has, by word or conscience, forbidden that offensive thought or deed.

** It is clear that the believer in the gospel is justified from *all* guilt at the moment of his conversion—both the personal guilt of his own trespasses as well as the imputed guilt that is inherited by all people from Adam. The Bible nowhere explains how a deceased infant can be justified from Adam's imputed guilt without having the opportunity or ability to repent and be converted. We are left, however, to acknowledge the tremendous focus of scripture on "known sins" as well as the oft-repeated basis of judgment "according to every man's works" (Matthew 16:27; 1 Peter 1:17; Revelation 20:13, etc.). These emphases, which are entirely irrelevant to infants, lead us to conclude that children who die in infancy are exceptional cases and recipients of exceptional mercies related to their inherited guilt from Adam.

Scripture Texts

Romans 4:15	*for where no law is, there is no transgression.*
Romans 5:13	*but sin is not imputed when there is no law.*
Romans 7:8	*But sin, taking occasion by the commandment, wrought in me all manner of concupiscence. For without the law sin was dead.*
Romans 7:9	*For I was alive without the law once: but when the commandment came, sin revived, and I died.*
James 4:17	*Therefore to him that knoweth to do good, and doeth it not, to him it is sin.*
2 Samuel 12:23	*But now he is dead, wherefore should I fast? can I bring him back again? I shall go to him, but he shall not return to me.*
Luke 18:15–17	*And they brought unto him also infants, that he would touch them: but when his disciples saw it, they rebuked them. But Jesus called them unto him, and said, Suffer little children to come unto me, and forbid them not: for of such is the kingdom of God. Verily I say unto you, Whosoever shall not receive the kingdom of God as a little child shall in no wise enter therein.*
Matthew 18:1–6	*At the same time came the disciples unto Jesus, saying, Who is the greatest in the kingdom of heaven? And Jesus called a little child unto him, and set him in the midst of them, And said, Verily I say unto you, Except ye be converted, and become as little children, ye shall not enter into the kingdom of heaven. Whosoever therefore shall humble himself as this little child, the same is greatest in the kingdom of heaven. And whoso shall receive one such little child in my name receiveth me. But whoso shall offend one of these little ones which believe in me, it were better for him that a millstone were hanged about his neck, and that he were drowned in the depth of the sea.*

ENDNOTES

Chapter 1

[1] Wesminster Shorter Catechism, Question 1.

[2] Philippians 1:21–23, English Standard Version (ESV)

Chapter 2

[1] Jess Connolly and Hayley Morgan, *Wild and Free: A Hope-Filled Anthem for the Woman Who Feels Like She is Both Too Much and Never Enough* (Grand Rapids, Mich.: Zondervan, 2016), 175.

[2] "Live," https://www.azlyrics.com/lyrics/nicholenordeman/live.html.

[3] Lysa Terkeurst, *What Happens When Women Say Yes to God: Experiencing Life in Extraordinary Ways* (Eugene, Ore.: Harvest House, 2007), 83.

Chapter 3

[1] Kristen Strong, *Girl Meets Change: Truths to Carry You Through Life's Transitions* (Grand Rapids, Mich.: Revell, 2015), 19.

Chapter 4

[1] Priscilla Shirer, *Life Interrupted: Navigating the Unexpected* (Nashville: B&H Publishing Group, 2011), 21.

[2] Jeremiah 29:5–6, ESV

[3] Jeremiah 29:11, Berean Study Bible

[4] Elizabeth George, *Loving God with All Your Mind Interactive Workbook* (Eugene, Ore.: Harvest House, 2010), 77.

[5] Hannah Hurnard, *Hinds Feet on High Places, Complete and Unabridged* (Blacksburg, Va.: Wilder Publications, 2010), 62.

Chapter 5

[1] John Piper, "George Mueller's Strategy for Showing God Simplicity of Faith, Sacred Scripture, and Satisfaction in God," https://www.desiringgod.org/messages/george-muellers-strategy-for-showing-god#35.

[2] Max Lucado, *In the Eye of the Storm: A Day in the Life of Jesus* (Nashville: Thomas Nelson, 1991), 50–52.

Chapter 6

[1] John MacArthur, *Safe in the Arms of God: Truth from Heaven About the Death of a Child* (Nashville: Thomas Nelson, 2003), 32.

[2] Mary Evelyn Smith, "On Abortion: Learning Empathy and Changing my Heart," http://www.whatdoyoudodear.com/on-abortion-learning-empathy-and/.

[3] Psalm 139:15–16, ESV

[4] "All of Me," https://www.lyricsmode.com/lyrics/m/matthew_hammitt/all_of_me.html.

[5] Ann Voskamp, *The Broken Way: A Daring Path into the Abundant Life* (Grand Rapids, Mich.: Zondervan, 2016), 131.

[6] Jessica Paulraj, "This is Motherhood{Too}: A *Very* Special Needs Adoption Journey," http://michaelaevanow.com/2014/07/15/this-is-motherhood-too-a-very-special-needs-adoption-journey/.

Chapter 7

[1] Charles Stanley, *How to Handle Adversity* (Nashville: Oliver-Nelson Books, 1989), 6.

[2] "Gateway to Joy Transcript from Back to the Bible," https://web.archive.org/web/20140727193826, http://www.backtothebible.org/index.php/Gateway-to-Joy/Do-the-Next-Thing.html.

[3] Mary Beth Chapman with Ellen Vaughn, *Choosing to SEE: A Journey of Struggle and Hope* (Grand Rapids: Revell, 2010), 187.

[4] C. S. Lewis, *A Grief Observed* (New York: Harper Collins, 1961), 29.

[5] Ali Gilkeson, Chris Llewellyn, Gareth Gilkeson, Stephen Mitchell, and Patrick Thompson, *Weep With Me*, Album: *Good News*, Capitol Christian Music Group, 2018. Lyrics accessed from Genius Lyrics, September 19, 2018, https://genius.com/Rend-collective-weep-with-me-lyrics.

Chapter 8

1. Vaneetha Rendall Risner, *The Scars That Have Shaped Me: How God Meets Us In Suffering* (Minneapolis: Desiring God, 2016), 40.
2. Psalm 6:2–3, 6:6–7
3. Vaneetha Rendall Risner, *The Scars That Have Shaped Me: How God Meets Us In Suffering* (Minneapolis: Desiring God, 2016), 36.
4. Ann Lamott, *Bird By Bird: Some Instructions on Writing and Life* (New York: Random House, 1994), 18.
5. Nancy Guthrie, *Holding Onto Hope: A Pathway Through Suffering to the Heart of God* (Carol Stream, Ill.: Tyndale House, 2002), 79.
6. Annie F. Downs, *Looking for Lovely: Collecting the Moments That Matter* (Nashville: B&H Publishing Group, 2016), 137–138.

Chapter 9

1. Jennifer Rothschild, *Lessons I Learned in the Dark: Steps to Walking by Faith Not by Sight* (Colorado Springs, Col.: Multnomah Books, 2002), 74.
2. Hannah Hurnard, *Hinds Feet on High Places, Complete and Unabridged* (Blacksburg, Va.: Wilder Publications, 2010), 92.
3. M. Clarene Shantz, *The Sun Still Shines* (self-published, 2010).
4. Jennifer Rothschild, "Do You Deserve Hell?" www.jenniferrothschild.com/do-you-deserve-hell/.

Chapter 10

1. Louisa M.R. Stead, "Tis So Sweet to Trust in Jesus," 1882.
2. "*Knees To The Earth*," http://www.metrolyrics.com/knees-to-the-earth-lyrics-watermark.html.
3. Sarah Rieke (producer), *Episode 13: The Discipline of Surrender*, https://itunes.apple.com/us/podcast/heart-lessons-podcast/id1090554878.
4. Vaneetha Rendall Risner, *The Scars That Have Shaped Me: How God Meets Us In Suffering* (Minneapolis: Desiring God, 2016), 105.
* While I did write these words in my journal, they are not original, but quoted from one of my favorite hymns, "Channels Only," by Mary M. Maxwell.
5. Philippians 1:29, ESV
6. Justin Taylor, "A Woman of Whom the World Was Not Worthy: Helen Roseveare (1925–2016)" https://www.thegospelcoalition.org/blogs/justin-taylor/a-woman-of-whom-the-world-was-not-worthy-helen-roseveare-1925-2016/.

Chapter 11

[1]   Isaac Watts, "When I Survey The Wondrous Cross," 1707.

[2]   Albert E. Brumley, "I'll Fly Away," 1929.

Chapter 12

[1]   Randy Alcorn, *Heaven* (Carol Stream, Ill.: Tyndale House, 2004), 73.

Chapter 13

[1]   Nancy Guthrie, *Holding Onto Hope: A Pathway Through Suffering to the Heart of God* (Carol Stream, Ill.: Tyndale House, 2002), 73–74.

[2]   "Not For A Moment (After All)," https://www.multitracks.com/songs/Vertical-Church-Band/Live-Worship-From-Vertical-Church/Not-For-A-Moment-(After-All)/.

[3]   Sarah Rieke (producer), *Episode 6: Breaking Through Darkness*, https://itunes.apple.com/us/podcast/heart-lessons-podcast/id1090554878.

Chapter 14

[1]   C. S. Lewis, *A Grief Observed* (New York: Harper Collins, 1961), 46.

[2]   Rainbow baby is a term that refers to a baby born shortly after the loss of a previous baby due to miscarriage, stillbirth, or death in infancy. This term is used because a rainbow typically follows a rainstorm, indicating the storm has passed and hope for clear skies is on the way.

[3]   Lysa Terkeurst and Shaunti Feldhan, *Made to Crave for Young Women: Satisfying Your Deepest Desires with God* (Grand Rapids, Mich.: Zondervan, 2012), 3.

Chapter 15

[1]   Ann Voskamp, *The Broken Way: A Daring Path into the Abundant Life* (Grand Rapids, Mich.: Zondervan, 2016), 20.

[2]   Angie Smith, *Mended: Pieces of A Life Made Whole* (Nashville: B&H Publishing, 2012), 8.

[3]   Sarah Rieke, "The Broken Pitcher," http://www.lifeandgrace.com/2014/01/the-broken-pitcher.html.

[4]   Jeremiah 18:6

Chapter 16

[1] 1 Rosalind Goforth, *How I Know God Answers Prayer* (Chicago: Moody Press, 1970), 8.

Chapter 18

[1] Jen Hatmaker, *Of Mess and Moxie: Wrangling Delight Out of This Wild and Glorious Life* (Nashville: Thomas Nelson Books, 2017), 249.

[2] Lucy Rodgers, David Gritten, James Offer, and Patrick Asare, "Syria: The Story of the Conflict," https://www.bbc.com/news/world-middle-east-26116868.

Chapter 20

[1] Unknown, https://www.facebook.com/photo.php?fbid=1130798 500281149&set=p.1130798500281149&type=3&theater.

[2] Annie F. Downs, *100 Days to Brave: Unlocking Your Most Courageous Self* (Grand Rapids, Mich.: Zondervan, 2017), 150.

Chapter 21

[1] Matthew 25:23, ESV

[2] Matthew 25:24–25, ESV

[3] "Nothing Is Wasted," https://www.azlyrics.com/lyrics/jasongray/nothingiswasted.html.

Chapter 22

[1] Franchesca Cox, *Celebrating Pregnancy Again: Restoring the Lost Joys of Pregnancy After the Loss of a Child* (CreateSpace Independent Publishing Platform, 2013), 43.

[2] "I Am Not Alone," https://genius.com/Kari-jobe-i-am-not-alone-lyrics.

Chapter 23

[1] Nancy Leigh DeMoss, *Lies Women Believe: And the Truth That Sets Them Free* (Chicago: Moody Publishers, 2001), 243.

[2] Ecclesiastes 4:9–10, ESV

Chapter 24

[1]   "Nothing But the Blood of Jesus," https://hymnary.org/text/
what_can_wash_away_my_sin.

Conclusion

[1]   Jordan Tate, *Just Keep Breathing: Unfiltered Thoughts on Life After Loss,
The Struggle of Grief, and Learning to Hope Again* (Bloomington, Ind.:
WestBow Press, 2017), 132–133.

[2]   Louisa M.R. Stead, "Tis So Sweet to Trust in Jesus," 1882.

Printed in the United States
By Bookmasters